# WALKING THE COTSWOLD WAY

# WALKING
# THE COTSWOLD WAY

June Lewis

**DAVID & CHARLES**
Newton Abbot   London   North Pomfret (Vt)

To my fellow Cotswold wardens who give so much of
themselves to so many things Cotswold

Line drawings and sketch maps by June Lewis

Labelling by Jennifer Johnson

**British Library Cataloguing in Publication Data**

Lewis, June R.
 Walking the Cotswold Way.
 1. Cotswold Way (England)  2. Cotswold Hills
 (England)—Description and travel—Guide-books
 I. Title
 914.24'1704858    DA670.C83

 ISBN 0-7153-8715-4

© June R. Lewis, 1986

Phototypeset by Typesetters (Birmingham) Ltd,
Smethwick, West Midlands
and printed in Great Britain
by Redwood Burn Limited, Trowbridge
for David & Charles Publishers plc
Brunel House   Newton Abbot   Devon

Published in the United States of America
by David & Charles Inc
North Pomfret   Vermont 05053   USA

# Contents

The author and publishers wish to emphasise that walkers should gain permission from the owner before entering any private property.

# Introduction

The Cotswold Way stretches for almost one hundred miles along the escarpment of the western edge of the Cotswold Hills, from the homely old market town of Chipping Campden in the north to the fashionable city of Bath in the south.

There is both unity and diversity in the Cotswold Way. Historically, it follows the story of Cotswold itself: from the rolling sheepwalks of the north wolds where heavy-fleeced Cotswold sheep flourished on the rich limestone herbage and made monasteries and merchants wealthy, through the steep sided valleys of the central region where the wool trade moved as cloth-making took over from sheep-farming, and on to the softer downlike parklands of the south wolds where Cotswold's ancient wool ties finally weakened as commerce looked to the Avon valley ports for a wider market. Geographically, the landscape reflects the historical progress, which to a great extent it also influenced.

Architecturally, the route starts with the mellowed wool-market buildings of the Middle Ages, moving on to the industrialised central steeps, where close-windowed mills line the valley bottoms and grand clothiers' houses ride the ridgeline, and through the landscaped country of the eighteenth century to arrive at the Georgian grace and Regency beauty of Bath.

The unifying element is the stone of Cotswold: in the geological Genesis when the great waters receded, the plateau of limestone on sand on clay tilted towards the Thames Valley and the westfacing escarpment emerged. The formation of this physical land barrier made a natural defence line for Cotswold's first settlers and ancient Iron Age hill forts punctuate the entire Way along the very backbone of the Cotswolds.

Erosion of the hill line over thousands of years has formed a dramatic, almost coastline scarp, with cliff bluffs and sweeping bays and inlet combes. Views from the heights are still of land, however, not seascapes, with a wide vista of vales and plains and the River Severn weaving its sinuous course parallel with the Way for a good forty miles or so.

The wayfarer is constantly reminded of the Cotswold's geological origin, but it is the use of the local stone which has given the whole area its unity: the oolitic limestone, soft enough when quarried to shape freely, hardens on exposure and seems to absorb the light mellowing and blending into the landscape so that it looks as if grown from it. Church, manor, barn, cottage, grand gatehouse and garden privy are all of a piece, all built of the same stone, and enclosed all round with the lesser ragstone walls – only size and situation separating one from another. Gabled roofs pitch steeply to carry the weight of the stone tiles, which are hung on pegs and overlap in graduated sizes so that they are as snugly-fitting and waterproof as the feathers on a bird's wing. Cotswold architecture is distinctive in style, born out of practicality of purpose, but even within the homogeneous whole there is diversity in design and local character. Regional variation in the minerals of the stone identify individual areas, the tonal qualities ranging from honey and cream to ochre and gold to pearly grey and silver white.

The escarpment is not just a remote ridgeway walk. The Cotswold Way follows footpaths and bridle tracks to seek out quiet villages and small market towns strung together with beautiful countryside, each with its own story like the charms on a necklace.

The wayfarer can be as alone as Adam on a remote hilltop with only the wind as companion, or one of a chattering crowd in a country pub, where the issue under discussion is more likely to be who cropped the earliest potatoes than national politics.

Parochial pride is very strong in the Cotswolds and accounts for tenacity to tradition; customs are an inherent part of Cotswold culture. A calendar of the most spectacular events is given, for it may be offputting for a wayfarer arriving at the foot of Cooper's Hill on a spring evening to face the onslaught of a Double Gloucester cheese and leggy lads hurtling down the steep slope in hot pursuit. It might seem that we do funny things with our local cheeses – Cotsall cooks slip a slice under the crust of our apple pies for as my grandfather used to say: 'an apple pie without the cheese, is like a kiss without the squeeze'.

Every village and town along the Way has something to offer in the social calendar – perhaps tea on the vicarage lawn, a barn dance at the farm, a recital in the manor, an exhibition of crafts, or a flower festival in the church; or there may be a Mop fair in the street, a feast on the village green, point-to-point or gymkhana, bonfire nights and general 'bun-fights', and at the end of the year the ancient ritualistic revelry and buffoonery of the Christmas Mummers.

Isolation or integration, the choice is the walker's. Stately houses, historic abbeys and a castle, country parks, working farms and legend-locked quarries, bustling market towns and ghost-ridden ruins; small museums crammed with yesterday, a working monastery in today's world, long barrows beyond the longest memory; secret combes and bold follies, whispering woods where badgers roam and primroses hide; misty dewponds and busy brooks, squeaky kissing gates and solid stone stiles, calm mill ponds and a motorway roundabout – the Cotswolds is a land of contrast. It is home to a pocketful of poets, and birthplace and resting place of some of history's great men.

The Cotswold Way is outstanding among the network of long-distance footpaths, not only for the sheer beauty and variety of its route, but for the fact that it is officially unofficial! It has never been designated by Act of Parliament an official long-distance footpath, so does not benefit from the maintenance grants and financial aid, and yet it is acknowledged to be the most comprehensive and effectively waymarked of all the long-distance routes in Great Britain.

Its very existence is due to the volunteer Cotswold wardens, who patient beings that they are, felt seventeen years a reasonable time to wait for a reply to their proposal for a footpath route along the western escarpment. The Gloucestershire Ramblers Association showed even more tolerance – they had first mooted the idea in the 1950s. Undeterred, and smiled on kindly by the County Council, the two bodies opened up the Cotswold Way themselves. Under the Gloucestershire County Council's recreational plan for the countryside, the Cotswold Way scheme was launched in 1970. Using existing public rights of way, and with the permission of over a hundred landowners, the Cotswold Wardens and the Gloucestershire ramblers waymarked the whole ninety-seven and a half mile route.

My own introduction to the Cotswold Way was during 'Operation Cotswaymark' when a group of my students worked with our Cotswold warden service surveying, plotting, detailing and helping to waymark a length of the Way for the service section of the Duke of Edinburgh award scheme.

The Cotswold warden service is a volunteer body, coordinated and administered by the head warden. Some 270 voluntary wardens work and care for the 600 square miles of the Cotswolds, which the Countryside Commission designated in 1966 as an area of outstanding natural beauty. Between them the wardens give some 24,000 hours of their time in any one year, the equivalent of fourteen full-time wardens, towards maintaining and enhancing the beauty of the Cotswold countryside and the quality of life for its residents and visitors.

Reconciling the often conflicting interests of landowners and tourists requires a delicate hand for it is essential that such a predominantly rural and agricultural area is safeguarded if it is to continue to be productive and conserve its tranquil charm, yet these are the very attractions which visitors come to the Cotswolds to experience.

Education, not confrontation, is the keynote of the service, although after a weekend's litter sweep collecting rusted bed-frames, car wheels, garden refuse, builders' rubble, chairs, fridges and all kinds of other material discarded by the human race, from hedgerows, ponds and beauty spots, our endearment for visitors wears a little thin – especially when some people have actually condoned dumping rubbish because 'those nice Cotswold Wardens will get rid of it'!

Maintenance, repair and improvement and clearance of foot-paths, hedge-laying, dry stone walling, draining, revetment, and stile-building require many hours of hard physical work. Patrol-ling takes up some one hundred man hours for each of the forty wardens who keep a watching brief on the Cotswold Way footpaths. Green-armbanded wardens are to be found on the recreational sites at Crickley, Coaley, Cooper's Hill, Fish Hill and Dyrham Park. They find lost children, organise car parking, man exhibitions or archaeological digs, identify a shrub or strap up a strained ankle; they are to be found planting trees and putting up signposts, painting waymarks in isolated spots and shepherding visitors on a farm open day; and they can also be found in a darkened village hall projecting an audio-visual story of a particular place.

Over the last decade the service has assembled a comprehen-sive record of village and town life in the region, which is of great historic and educational value. Interpreting the area has become an increasing aspect of the service: from the first tentative guided walk when four wardens took one visiting soul round a village, explaining its history and ecology, to the results of a concentrated publicity drive which brought out over two hundred walkers for the next lone warden. Experience and organisation have evened the odds somewhat and the wardens now guide around 120 walks throughout the year, attracting some 4,200 people.

The programme of walks, available free through libraries, is varied in content and distance: ranging from one for those of us who are charmed out of our beds to hear the dawn chorus in the depths of a Cotswold wood, to the newly-introduced week-long walk along the Cotswold Way; both have proved so popular that tickets for them are strictly limited.

The popularity of the Cotswold Way is not entirely due to its classification as a long-distance footpath – although figures, which are progressively increasing, indicate that approximately 8,000 people each year walk it in whole or part. Its charm rests in offering itself to be sampled in whole or part. Like a heady old wine it can be consumed in one long continuous draught for an intoxicating sense of achievement, or stepped and sipped at so that each section is an exhilarating experience leaving a warm glow in its wake and a tantalising taste of what lies ahead.

The Cotswold Way is a walk for all seasons which attracts people for a variety of purposes. We met walkers wandering and pondering, strolling and striding; a few resolute and regulated to a rigid time-table, backpacked and neither deviating from the way, nor stopping to listen to birds on the bough or smell the scent of summer rain on sun-baked stone. Some were southward bent on Bath, others northward charmed to Chipping Campden. Both directions offer challenges and compensations: to go south-wards is like walking through history; to go northwards is to have the characteristics of the Cotswolds unfold before you with the comfort of the prevailing wind at your back. Most walked only a section at a time, for the route allows for such selection being easily reached from many points with access to public transport or car parking.

Time and circumstance often permitted my sister Edna (whom I refer to as Nen) and I, but a couple of miles progress at a time – though we walked twice that distance, having to retrace our steps to where we had left the car.

Walking throughout the changing seasons of the year gave the walk extra dimension and provided added interest for 'The

Countryside', the Radio 4 programme which recorded some of our walks along the Way. It may have been coincidence, but following closely on the broadcast of one of the programmes, the *Daily Telegraph* radio critic wrote: 'One of the reasons people grow fond of Radio 4, so fond they fear for it and grow protective about it in a close and clannish way, is that it is full of people talking enthusiastically to you about peculiar things.'

This is a personalised account of our Walk, but the peculiar thing is that you too may be just as enthusiastic about it when you discover the pleasure, peace and cultural charm of this precious part of our countryside.

So welcome to our beautiful part of the world and to the way of Cotswold which awaits you on the Cotswold Way.

# Cotswaymark and Country-care Codes

## Operation Cotswaymark

'The best waymarked long-distance footpath in Britain', say the appreciative letters which are received by the Head Cotswold Warden. He also receives the brickbats for any lapses in this standard which is such a source of pride in a completely voluntary service. For it is through the unstinting goodwill of some thirty volunteer wardens that the Cotswold Way is so effectively waymarked that it is possible to follow the whole route without the aid of a map.

The more prudent, practical or plain pessimistic will, of course, pack a pile of maps into their backpacks and spend more time checking their grid references than enjoying the scenery. Whilst having the greatest respect, even awe, of the cartographer's craft from my attempt to simplify the graphical route by means of strip maps, I have listed (page 16) only the Ordnance Survey maps which set the route in perspective of the region; thus the Way is set in the context of the Cotswolds, instead of being an isolated perambulation along a precarious scarp slope.

Operation Cotswaymark was started in 1975. The joint efforts of the Cotswold Warden Service and the Ramblers' Association meant the universal system, recommended by the Countryside Commission, was used to denote rights of way. Thus:

**Footpaths** are indicated by *yellow arrows*.

**Bridleways** which, properly interpreted, mean a right of way on horseback, on pushbike and on foot, are shown by *blue arrows*.

**The Cotswold Way**, indicated by *white arrows* followed by *a white spot* (the size of a tenpenny piece), supplements and enlarges upon the national code. This is particularly useful when several rights of way converge. *Headless arrows* are painted at particularly difficult path junctions, the stems emulating the directions in which paths branch out – only the *Cotswold Way*

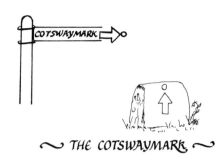

~ THE COTSWAYMARK ~

stem ends in an *arrowhead*. The *white spot* becomes a *target disc* at points where the route crosses, for example, a cultivated field.

Circular and other specific routes on occasion criss-cross and diverge from points along the Cotswold Way. These are specially planned walks and trails devised and waymarked by the Cotswold Warden Service as part of their continuing programme of guided walks. Although their signs should not be confusing to any walker bent on walking the Cotswold Way following the white arrows and spots, it is worth explaining a few of the strange symbols here, not only to aid elimination, but as a reminder of the many pleasant routes which radiate from the different areas en route. Thus, circular routes, for which there are printed booklets, are indicated by an *arrow with a coloured tail*; Stroud Valley walks are distinguished by a *yellow spot*; Witcombe Woods bridle-trails are shown by a *horseshoe blaze*, and the Wychavon Way, which branches out from Winchcombe into the heart of Worcestershire, has a distinguishing *golden crown*.

It is the policy of the Warden Service to utilise as many existing surfaces as possible and not to litter the countryside with extra furniture for waymarking. The white arrows and spots are therefore painted on gateposts and fences and trees where possible, although rough-barked trunks present a problem. In towns and villages, they are often to be found on the upright part of kerbstones, or on a metal post serving some other utilitarian purpose. Sharpening the observation heightens the route-finder's desire for exploration to spot the spots. And one should also show some degree of tolerance towards those few misguided pranksters who take some form of pleasure from turning signposts round, and the odd wayward cattle which lick off freshly painted signs – we, as Cotswold Wardens, do care for the latter creatures as well as our fellows, so the paint is specifically non-toxic!

## The Country Code

Caring for the countryside is really a code of conduct, common-sense and concern for others, their property, the flora and fauna and the environment itself, embodied in The Country Code:

Guard against all risks of fire. Remember that a glass bottle on a dried-grass patch attracts the sun's rays and can ignite. Fasten all gates properly; 'fasten' is different from 'close'. Keep dogs under strict control – it is senseless to specify 'at lambing time' – sheep have weaker hearts than most other animals and chasing them at any time of the year causes distress and can lead to death. There is a high penalty now for any form of sheep worrying.

Keep to the designated footpaths across farmland. If you are in doubt, ask if possible, and apologise if too late to ask! You can't claim the excuse of 'I'm on the Cotswold Way' as an inherent right; it is a privilege which was sought and fought for – that everyone and anyone should have a right of passage, not trespass, from one right of way proper to another.

Avoid damage to fences, hedges and walls. Their obvious function is to keep livestock in, but they also constitute property in themselves, so please don't create short cuts through and over them. Apart from unsightly and costly damage, such thoughtless action can disrupt the habitat of innumerable small wildlife.

Avoid litter. We are not asking you to take it home; there are litter bins at picnic sites and in all the villages and towns. Apart from its ugliness there is danger from broken bottles, plastic bags and jagged tins, not only to livestock but to fellow walkers.

Safeguarding water supplies is only common decency; streams and ponds and rivers are not open drains. Much relies on them and therefore much can be destroyed.

Care on a country road is essential. The scene may look like sleepy valley, but the road goes to and from somewhere, and somebody may be on their way.

Protect the wildlife and the environment, please! There are heavy penalties for contravening the Wildlife and Countryside Act of 1981. Briefly, it is breaking the law to uproot *any* wild plant without the landowner's consent. Specially protected rare plants may not be picked, let alone uprooted, or sold. *All* wild birds, their nests and eggs have special protection. Disturbance of certain butterflies and mammals, and specified species such as the great-crested newt, is illegal.

The countryside is so special, increasingly precious and very vulnerable. You could destroy it, but I'm sure will not. Because it is just not the Cotswold Way to do so.

## Maps covering the Cotswold Way

Ordnance Survey Landranger Series 1:50,000
Sheet No 151 Stratford-upon-Avon
            150 Worcester and the Malverns
            163 Cheltenham and Cirencester
            162 Gloucester and Forest of Dean
            172 Bristol and Bath

The increasing popularity of the Cotswold Way as a long-distance footpath has stimulated putting forward for consideration such improvements as may qualify for grant-aid for what is now termed a recreational footpath. Therefore a re-survey of the entire route is currently being carried out to assess any major physical problems and re-routing requirements which could benefit from financial assistance from the Countryside Commission. The scale of the sketch maps at the beginning of each chapter is approximately 2¼in to 1 mile. Proposals for re-routing are at present in hand for the following sections:

*Lower Goscombe to Stumps Cross, to achieve a safer route (map, page 43)

*Cleeve Common: re-routing over the north and west side and on top of the scarp (by courtesy of the Cleeve Common Conservators), rather than on the original route along the definitive bridleway below (map, page 67)

*Seven Springs: re-routing is planned for the north approach so as to avoid a horrendous mile of road walking (map, page 73)

*Ryeford area in the Stroud Valley, together with Selsey Common (map, page 102)

These proposals are shown in the relevant strip maps, but do bear in mind that, because the overriding concern of the Cotswold Warden Service is the safety and enjoyment of the public, improvements, which may involve re-routing, are an ongoing project.

THE WAYMARKED ROUTE IS THE CORRECT ONE.

# Progressive Mileage
## along the Cotswold Way

The chart on the following page gives the distance between Chipping Campden, the start, and various points along the route, thus allowing the walker a ready guide from which to plan individual walks along the way. Together with the aid of the strip maps, it is possible to do the walk in short sorties, as car parking is usually quite easy at, or near, the different points. Shown below are the most commonly seen mileage posts along the route.

To BATH
XCVII
miles

CAMPDEN
50 MILES

BATH
81 kms

~ COTSWOLD WAY ~
MILEAGE MARKS

To
CHIPPING
CAMPDEN

100 miles

| | Km | (Miles) | | Km | (Miles) |
|---|---|---|---|---|---|
| Broadway | 8.8 | (5.5) | Coaley Peak | 90.9 | (56.5) |
| Stanton | 16.1 | (10) | Frocester Hill | 91.7 | (57) |
| Stanway | 18.5 | (11.5) | crossroads | | |
| Stumps Cross | 20.9 | (13) | Crawley Hill | 93.3 | (58) |
| Hailes Abbey | 24.1 | (15) | Cam Long Down | 94.9 | (59) |
| Winchcombe | 28.2 | (17.5) | Dursley | 97.4 | (60.5) |
| Belas Knap | 33.0 | (20.5) | Stinchcombe Hill | 100.6 | (62.5) |
| Cleeve Hill | 37.0 | (23) | North Nibley | 103.8 | (64.5) |
| (Youth Hostel) | | | Tyndale Monument | 105.4 | (65.5) |
| Puckham crossroads | 41.8 | (26) | Wotton-under-Edge | 108.6 | (67.5) |
| Dowdeswell | 45.1 | (28) | Blackquarries Hill | 112.7 | (70) |
| (Reservoir Inn) | | | Alderley | 115.1 | (71.5) |
| Seven Springs | 49.1 | (30.5) | Somerset Monument | 119.9 | (74.5) |
| Leckhampton Hill | 52.3 | (32.5) | Hawkesbury Upton | 120.7 | (75) |
| Ullenwood crossroads | 54.7 | (34) | Horton | 123.9 | (77) |
| Crickley Hill | 58.7 | (36.5) | Old Sodbury | 127.9 | (79.5) |
| Birdlip | 62.0 | (38.5) | Dodingon Park | 129.5 | (80.5) |
| Cooper's Hill | 66.0 | (41) | Tormarton Interchange | 132.8 | (82.5) |
| Fiddler's Elbow | 66.8 | (41.5) | (M4) | | |
| Painswick Beacon | 70.0 | (43.5) | Dyrham Park | 136.8 | (85) |
| Painswick | 72.4 | (45) | Pennsylvania (on A46) | 139.2 | (86.5) |
| Edgemoor Inn | 74.8 | (46.5) | Cold Ashton | 140.8 | (87.5) |
| (on A4173) | | | (on A46 at Turn) | | |
| Haresfield Beacon | 78.9 | (49) | Granville Monument | 144.8 | (90) |
| Westrip | 83.7 | (52) | Prospect Stile | 148.9 | (92.5) |
| Ryeford (on A419) | 85.3 | (53) | Weston, Penn Hill Road | 151.3 | (94) |
| Middle Yard | 87.7 | (54.5) | Bath (at Abbey) | 156.1 | (97) |

# 1
# Chipping Campden to Broadway

The new year was only hours old when we arrived at Chipping Campden to begin our walk on the Cotswold Way. This properly starts – or finishes, depending on which direction you walk it – on the south-west edge of the town, but with all the Cotsaller's pride in their own land I wanted to show off the lovely old market town to the BBC who were to record extracts of our progress throughout the four seasons. With all the dignity and medieval charm which has earned it such glowing titles as the 'jewel in the Cotswold's crown', Chipping Campden looked magnificent as the early mist cleared to allow a high-riding January sun to flood the broad street with a clarity of light, golden from where it was glancing off the honey-coloured buildings but pointing doorways, undereaves and the nooks and crannies between the tall chimneys and swept valleys of the stone-tiled houses with deep shadow. The early hoar frost edged the grass with crystal and a colony of rooks 'cyawed' their interest from the churchyard trees – in deference to our presence there rather than that of the 200-year-old limes honouring the twelve apostles.

The parish church of Chipping Campden makes a significant and historic point from which to start the journey in the north towards the goal of Bath Abbey in the south. Vastly different in style and environs, both are monuments to the Cotswold craftsmen's skill in stone. The church at Chipping Campden is also a testimonial to the wool trade which brought such prosperity to the Cotswold area for so many centuries.

The Norman invaders found an already thriving wool industry where the Saxons had made use of this fertile sheltered *campus* in the vale of the high wolds and developed a brisk export trade with their homeland so that, by the twelfth century, the popular saying was:

In Europe the best wool is English,
In England the best wool is Cotswold.

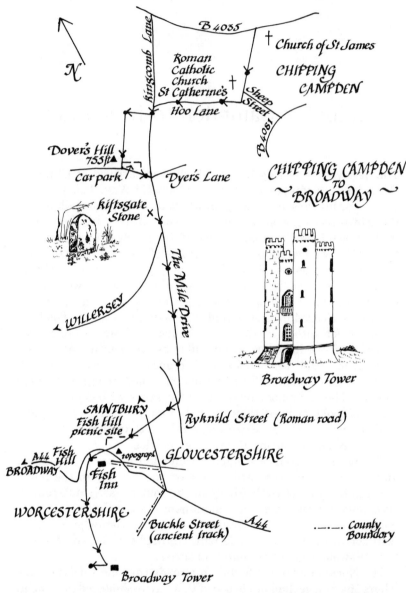

The map shows the route from Chipping Campden to Broadway, including: N (compass), B 4035, Kinscomb Lane, Roman Catholic Church St Catherine's, Church of St James, CHIPPING CAMPDEN, Sheep Street, Hoo Lane, B 4081, Dover's Hill 755ft, Car park, Dyer's Lane, Kiftsgate Stone, The Mile Drive, WILLERSEY, Broadway Tower, CHIPPING CAMPDEN TO BROADWAY, SAINTBURY Fish Hill picnic site, Ryknild Street (Roman road), GLOUCESTERSHIRE, A44 Fish Hill, BROADWAY, Fish Inn, topograph, WORCESTERSHIRE, Buckle Street (ancient track), A44, County Boundary, Broadway Tower

Broadway Tower

Broadway Tower

The dominance of Cotswold wool dictated the politics of the day and such was its importance in the continental courts that an act prohibiting the export of sheep, without licence from the king, was passed in 1434. A special request for sixty sacks of 'beste Cotteswoolle' was made by the King of Portugal for making cloth of gold for court ceremonial dress. In gratitude for the white lustrous fleeces which turned to gold in the medieval markets, the Lord High Chancellor sank down thankfully on a woolsack in Parliament, and wealthy woolmerchants raised up noble churches in the Cotswolds. The woolsack and the 'wool' churches are enduring legacies of the Age of the Golden Fleece.

St James's is one of the finest of the Cotswold 'wool' churches. Rebuilt in the Perpendicular style in the fifteenth century, it has a unity of design which is quite unusual in our country churches. The greatest benefactor was William Grevel, who was accorded the largest and one of the earliest of the many memorial brasses in Gloucestershire to carry the emblematic epitaph 'the flower of wool merchants of all England'. Even the elaborate alabaster tableaux of the Sir Baptist Hicks's family, who held the Manor in the seventeenth century and were so incredibly rich that James I borrowed 'on several occasions' from them, fail to eclipse the import of the woolmerchant in the story of Campden. The church itself is a treasure house of art. Elegant sculptures and simple stone masonry vie for attention with the beautiful velvet cope enriched with the figures of saints and golden roses embroidered in the time of Richard II, and the exquisitely stitched altar cloths of white silk damask, some 500 years old, which were copied for the High Altar of Westminster Abbey for the coronation of George V. Ancient records of the church are exhibited in the small muniments room, once used as a schoolroom.

But scant reference to the church and its treasures could be afforded as we announced to Radio 4 listeners who and where we were, as the bell-ringers assembled to start us off to a merry peal on the 300-year-old bells. Then I asked George Hart, Campden

Church of St James

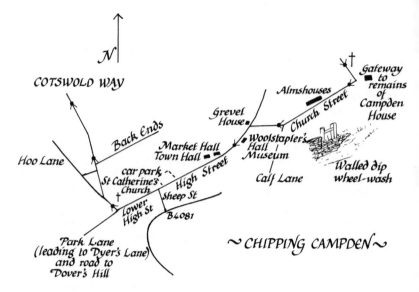

born and bred, if he and his fellows had given up the age-old habit of shin-kicking and clouting each other with cudgels at the Dover's Games in the Cotswolds. As Jethro of *The Archers*, George was not at all inhibited by the microphone under his nose, and spoke about the Scuttlebrook Wake and his childhood days at the old grammar school, itself a close contemporary of the church. We moved off in brisk fashion along the stony edge of the church path for the benefit of the sound effects and were excited no end when we listened with Caroline Elliot, our producer, to the playback, and grinned congratulatory grins at one another on how purposeful our footsteps sounded.

Beside the church are the remains of Campden House. The sweeping arched gateway with its pair of solid stone-roofed lodges, the finials of their cleverly constructed chimneys giving a touch of fantasy to the corner, is an elegant drop curtain behind which all the swashbuckling Jacobean manorial life was played out. But behind is an empty stage. The truth about how the magnificent mansion was destroyed is buried with the rebels of the Civil War and in the doubting corners of the historian's mind. From the back of the church along the Shipston road where Dick Smith farms fruit on Vale scale – the first PYO farm in the Cotswolds – can be seen two pavilions, thought to be summer-houses, either end of a terrace standing isolated in a field – silent sentinels to a turbulent past.

However grand the great house was, it could bear no comparison with the almhouses which Sir Baptist Hicks built opposite in 1612 to house six poor men and six poor women. However humble in intent, the houses are architectural gems, even by Chipping Campden's outstanding standards. For here is the epitome of Cotswold stone-masonry, superb craftsmanship in the vernacular. The symmetry on the plan of the letter 'I', which historians interpret as a mark of respect to Sir Baptist's monarch master, James I, the steeply pitched gables, elegant tall chimneys and deep mullioned windows, exude a dignified charm in domestic design. A raised pavement sets them properly apart from the road. Directly opposite is a wheel-wash where the coaches and carts of yesteryear were run into a water-filled walled dip, not so much to wash their wooden wheels as to soak them to prevent them drying out and splitting.

There is much to keep one at this spot but, as my sister, Nen, reminded us and listeners of Radio 4, we had 100 miles (160km) ahead of us and 'Cotswold miles be long 'uns'. So we followed Church Street to the sound of the eight bells after which the old inn at the bottom – already 100 years old when it housed the masons who built the church – is named.

The High Street offers yet more to detain the visitor. Turn left to follow the broad and long street, but look across to Grevel House on the right; with its stone tracery and gargoyles it is so little changed over six hundred years that one expects to see the woolpacked horses emerge through the ancient arched doorway. I wondered, as we passed by, whether the hoary old spirit of William Grevel would be with us hoping to meet again the Wife of Bath, for it is generally thought that the merchant in *The Canterbury Tales* was based on William Grevel. Chaucer was then under the patronage of John of Gaunt who lived in a corner of the vast sheep-walks of the Cotswolds, so it is certain that the prominent woolmerchants of the day would have been known to him. That Grevel 'so doon other mo that wedded been' is evidenced by his memorial brass which shows his 'wyf'; but it is impossible to tell whether she was 'a shrewe at al', for the artist paid more attention to detailing the eighty buttons on her dress than delineating her countenance.

Contemporary with Grevel House is Woolstapler's Hall opposite, built for Robert Calf, another wealthy woolmerchant, whose name is perpetuated in the lane running parallel behind the High Street. The Hall is now a museum and Tourist

Information Centre, so visitors to the town collect their accommodation lists and bus time-tables in the company of a fine fairground horse and in front of a fourteenth-century fireplace. The original hall where the merchants dealt in their wool wares, is upstairs, and houses such diverse curios as mantraps and a Victorian balloon and parachute.

C. R. Ashbee, who bought the Hall when he moved his Guild of Handicrafts to the town in 1902, restored it sympathetically, its purpose having long ceased following Campden's abortive attempt to be a Staple town. When it was refused its petition, it could no longer continue its former wool-trading. Ashbee 'signed' his name by means of a pun on it by incorporating an ash tree and bee in the stained-glass window which he put into the Hall.

Ashbee's Arts and Crafts Movement injected a much-needed awareness and rediscovery of old skills in a new machine-orientated age, and although it was short-lived its effect is long lasting, for the work and influence of those skilled artists manifests itself in the continuity of fine craftsmanship which is the soul of Cotswold tradition and which is displayed in no better setting than in this old wool town.

'History in stone' is the town's motto – most aptly illustrated in the long High Street, whose medieval mellowness mixes happily with Regency elegance. The ages of change are captured in a timber frame or a chamfered quoin and in many a telling name – Kings Arms Pantry, Poppett's Alley, Malt House, Badgers Hall, and Twine House – with the gabled Jacobean market hall holding the centre stage next to the Town Hall of ancient foundation. The prefix 'Chipping' is derived from the word for a market; Campden obtained its charter in 1180, and the shape of the town evolved as a clever piece of planning by the old burgesses to draw custom to and through it. By following the contour on the lee side of the Cotswold escarpment, both the monotony of a very long straight street and the draughty passageway it could have created have been avoided.

One, certainly not insignificant, piece of history seems to be ignored, however. Jonathan Hulls of Darby House, the local clock-repairer who invented the steamboat, has never been accorded the fame and status of other inventors. Maybe it was because the boat he built at Chipping Campden fell apart during trials on the River Avon at Evesham, and was lampooned by a local pen:

Jonathan Hull, with his paper skull,
Tried to make a machine to go 'gainst wind and stream,
But he, like an ass, couldn't bring it to pass
So at last was ashamed to be seen.

Hull himself had already written that an inventor 'too often meets with ridicule and contempt' – but worse perhaps is disregard. The prototype failed through lack of finance and therefore substantial materials, not design. Pamphlets describing his boat, sold at sixpence a copy in the coffee-houses, added only a little to his meagre resources, so the little steam-driven tug – many of its component parts directly related to the parts of a clock – which was to be his 'new-invented Machine for carrying Vessels or Ships out of, or into, any Harbour, Port or River against Wind or Tide, or in a Calm', was constructed with cheap wood and rope. Jonathan Hulls may not be a name hailed locally, but his design, patented in 1738, is acknowledged by the British Museum who added a note to his specifications that he gave the honour of inventing the steam-boat to England.

As the High Street tapers away on its curving line, a final reminder of its past catches the eye in the nameplate 'Sheep Street'. A little way down that street is the old silk mill where Ashbee centred his Guild of Handicrafts, giving yet another lease of life to one of the last of the mills to be built specifically for supplying the Coventry ribbon trade. When that trade declined, silk-throwing at Campden ceased. The mill then turned to glove- and stay-making until Ashbee and his craftsmen from White-chapel came at the turn of the century. Of Campden's early crafts, only the famous Hart family of silversmiths remain, working at the same old curved benches, nicked and notched from years of work, hung about with the traditional leather aprons to catch the precious silver shavings. As we crossed over the little junction, David Hart passed us, waving, for he and his band of ringers had just finished the peal – most of which was captured for ever on the BBC tape – and now he was returning to his Dickensian-type workshop at the top of the old mill to finish the chain of office for my home town's mayor. I felt more than a little pride in the fact that it was the coat-of-arms of the old wool-family of Tame, my paternal ancient ancestors, which had been chosen for the badge; for we, like Campden, grew up on wool.

At the end of the High Street a right-hand turn by St

Catherine's Church leads to Back Ends and Hoo Lane. A tall signpost announces the start of the Cotswold Way. A picture-postcard thatched cottage, a not altogether rare feature in this native-stone built and tiled land, makes an attractive starting point. Hoo Lane bears left, then narrows to a bridleway towards the top. A lady picking Brussels sprouts in a field, on the shoulder of the hill, chatted a moment. 'Time was I'd be just 'ere with meself', she said, and I marked her as local for we Cotsallers are never 'alone'. I don't know whether my explanation that the increased foot traffic up and down the Hoo was due to the opening up of the Cotswold Way aroused or allayed her intimated fears that the hill would be worn away if it went on at this rate – sometimes as many as a dozen walkers a day!

The rise of 200ft (60m) is the first introduction to the escarpment; but it is not until you have turned left onto Kingcomb Lane for a few yards, then followed the signpost through a gap in the hedge on the right, walked alongside the field and over the stile onto Dover's Hill, that you can appreciate the expansive views that the Cotswold ridgeway affords. From the very scarp edge the Cotswold hills can be seen reaching their most northern point, softly hued farmland floods the Vale of Evesham below, with the Malverns a hazy blue hill-ridge on the horizon. The route follows the line of trees leading left and westward, but it is more interesting to walk along the scarp edge: a topograph sets the geographical points in context.

Dover's Hill perpetuates the name of Robert Dover who 'being full of activity, and of a generous, free and public spirit, did with leave from King James I select a place on Cotswold Hills whereon games should be acted'. The games became known as the 'Cotswold Olympicks', and attracted the noble and notable of the day to the athletic sports and hare-coursing. The rougher antics of the peasants were leavened with an Ordinary each day of the Whitsuntide week at the Noel Arms, balls and concerts at the George while 'A Main of Cock's' fought each morning at the Green Dragon. Shakespeare was familiar with the games by his reference in *The Merry Wives of Windsor*, when Shallow asks, 'How does your fallow greyhound, sir? I heard say he was outrun on Cotsall.'

Endymion Porter, servant to the king, presented to Dover a suit 'of the King's old cloaths, with a hat and feather and ruff, purposely to grace him and consequently the solemnity'. The attendance of Prince Rupert in 1636 set a royal seal of approval to the 'famed Cotswold Sports and manly Diversions, not easily to be described', which were immortalised in poetry in a collection published that same year, entitled *Annalia Dubrensia*. In this, thirty-three poets eulogise the games and their founder. Ben Jonson's 'Epigram to my joviall good friend, Mr Robert Dover, on his great instauration of his hunting and dancing on Cotswold' is one of many from whose flowery phrases the sports earned the title 'Olympic':

> I cannot bring my Muse to dropp Vies
> Twixt Cotswold, and the Olimpicke exercise:
> But I can tell thee Dover, how they Games
> Renew the Glories of our blessed Jeames;
> How they doe keepe alive his memorie
> With the Glad Countrey and Posteritie.
> How they advance true Love and neighbourhood,
> And doe both Church and Common wealth the good,
> In spite of Hipocrites, who are the worst
> Of Subjects; Let such envie, till they burst.

Dover admitted in a 68 line poem to his 'Poeticall and Learned Noble Friends' who compiled the book, that he could not

> . . . tell what plannet rul'd when I
> First undertooke this mirth, this jollitie
> Nor can I give account to you at all,
> How this conceit into my braine did fall.

Political undertones obviously prompted the publication of *Annalia Dubrensia*, because Dover is on the defensive when he himself compares the baseness of the 'Sports and Playes' of ancient Greece with the 'sprightfull youth at exercise with the Pipe and Pot the only prise', ending his piece with:

> Let snarling Envie borke, pine, and grow mad:
> Let carping *Momus* powting bee, and sad,
> And let Content and Mirth all those attend,
> That doe all harmlesse honest sports defend.

Dover's son, as a captain of horse in Prince Rupert's army, found himself fighting for real on the hill during the Civil War, which put a stop to the games, but the 'Ancient Pastimes so justly fam'd' were revived at the Restoration and went from strength to strength. In 1806 a purse of 10 guineas was awarded to the team of eleven men who won at backswords, a gold-laced hat was wrestled for, gloves and ribands were danced for, a good pair of shoes were jumped for in 'Bags by Men', and a donkey race and 'Rural Sports to enumerate which wou'd fill a Volume' were offered 'to the Company which is expected to be more numerous and respectable than have assembled since their institution'.

The 'respectable' were finally deterred from the games by the mid-1800s, by which time horse-racing had been introduced and all the riff-raff of the industrialised Midlands, and railway navvies, descended on the quiet Cotswold town wreaking havoc and mayhem with their pick-pocketing, drunkenness, brawling and general debauchery. A bill passed through Parliament stopped the games after the event of 1851, which some 30,000 people attended; the Enclosure Act a couple of years later physically divided the hill, so what we now walk is but a part of the ancient hilltop amphitheatre.

As the games stopped, the importance of the Scuttlebrook Wake fair increased, but the flame of the old 'Olympicks' could not be extinguished. Its spirit lingered on and was finally fanned into life again in 1966 when the Robert Dover's Games Society revived the traditional sports. And so the ghosts of games past and times present are one when cavaliers and morris dancers and backswordists mingle with the locals and tourists each Spring bank holiday on the eve of the Scuttlebrook Wake.

The hill was given to the National Trust by a group of prominent writers and artists inspired by their friend Frederick Griggs whose artistic works are known throughout the Cotswolds. And as you come to the Trust's car park at the far end, look for the collection box, for on it is a picture of Dover in the plumed hat and king's clothes which he wore to open and preside over his 'Olympicks'. It is in this role that he is remembered because, according to an anonymous poet, as an attorney (his professional career) Dover never tried 'but two causes, having always made up the difference'.

From the car park the route turns left, then right at the crossroads marked Willersey and Broadway. The road-walking is relieved after about ½ mile (.8km) by looking for the Kiftsgate

Stone at the beginning of Weston Park wood on the right-hand side. An irregularly shaped stone, encrusted with lichen and with a small hole in its face, its significance derives from its purpose rather than its presentation, for it marked the moot point of the old Saxon hundred when 'gate' indicated a track. Everyone in the locality would have made tracks to the Kiftsgate Stone for all important business of the day, whether it was the sentence of a local felon or the proclamation of a king. The stone looks so at home in the woodland that it would be natural to think it had been there a thousand years; but in 1878 it was on the top of Dover's Hill, and it was said that it would be 'enclosed with a fence and a brass plate placed on it with description', so it was evidently moved from where it marked the boundary of the Kiftsgate boundary after that date together with the old stone seat, fairly close by. The stone is neither enclosed nor marked with a plate.

A little further on, the route leaves the road to follow the chestnut trees on the left and on to The Mile Drive; attractive in all seasons, but particularly so when the wild dog roses of summer knit together the different hedgerow shrubs. The avenue was probably landscaped in the latter half of the nineteenth century for the Earls of Gainsborough while they were living at Campden House. Beyond The Drive the walk crosses the course of Ryknild Street, then leads across two fields – muddy and rutted or waist-high in wheat according to the time of year. Another Roman road, Buckle Street, is crossed to enter Worcestershire, the field track continues to Fish Hill picnic site, landscaped from an old quarry. A topograph at the western tip points out the views from the picnic area – a fitting memorial to the late Don Russell whose scheme it was. A woodland trail from that point makes a pleasant diversion, and is indicative of the interest the Worcestershire Nature Conservation Trust has in this area. Sunny days reveal the secrets of the countryside hereabouts where orchids and harebells abound; while twilight taunts the senses in the deep cutting close by, known as Campden Hole, where restless ghosts roam free. Quarrying is active on the opposite side of the busy A44, and it is to the quarrymen that the notice to leave dirty boots outside the pub is directed, rather than to walkers; although we did make sure we cleaned ours of mud before we went inside what must be one of the quaintest of our many quaint country pubs.

The Fish Inn
Broadway

The Fish Inn is curious as well as quaint. It was first granted its licence as an inn by royal charter under the seal of Charles II. It was rebuilt in the mid-eighteenth century as a gazebo for the squire of Farncombe House, and became the haunt of the gay blades of the time to rendezvous over pipe and pot and a game of bowls. The old bowling green is now the inn's car park. The Reverend Richard Graves of Mickleton who was taught his Latin by Utrecia Smith, the curate's daughter, was a great friend of the eighteenth-century poet Shenstone and for his pleasure planted an avenue to lead to Kiftsgate which, together with neighbouring Hidcote, are famous gardens in the north Cotswolds. Shenstone composed his 'Ode to Ophelia' in honour of the 'blue-stocking' Utrecia, and Graves composed his 'Ode to the Fish' in honour of the old inn:

> Lo! here a Fish; high floating in the air,
> Bespeaks, you'll say, within but slender fare;
> Yet enter courteous guests, rest here and dine:
> The Fish shall spout good ale, good punch, good wine.
> If out of element our Fish appear,
> You think the towering falcon should be here,
> Cast but your eyes the vast expanse around,
> Within this tract all elements abound.

Fish certainly seem 'out of element' in this open countryside cut through by the traffic-teaming A44, following closely on the old serpentine road of the London to Worcester coach run. That the name, however, is of some importance can be judged by the hill being called after it. Tradition puts the roots of the inn much further back in antiquity – back to a monastic foundation of the fourteenth century, when the fish was used as a Christian symbol.

Mine hosts, Mr and Mrs Layton, are local folk, so happily the inn is free from the pseudo-country trappings that many new-comers to the Cotswolds think is necessary – and so, of course, it retains its genuine charm. The dining room reveals its age to those who care about the cut of stone and the hewing of timbers. It is said to be haunted, and Mrs Layton seemed slightly disappointed that she has not seen the ghost; but visitations of Public Health officials are quite enough for her to contend with for they find it hard to reconcile originality with regulations, so it is not without effort that the Fish retains its honest stone and wood when others would have cement and plastic. I was at once curious about the large fish shown in relief on a stone in the fireplace for, despite its fresh paint, it appeared old. Like the landlady, I believe this could be the headstone of the carp which the monks of old could not catch. For when it died of old age – it was reputed to be a hundred years old – it was buried nearby and a headstone was erected to its memory.

Mrs Layton remembers her uncle telling her that the landlord used to take the beer outside for the driver of the Royal Mail coach, who would stand on the inn steps so that he fulfilled his brief of never leaving the mail unattended. Extra horses were engaged to haul coaches up the long, and originally much steeper, Fish Hill; but the old stone inscribed 'Shut off two horses here' is now built into a gateway farther along the hill. The Laytons still hold a licence to sell water at a shilling a bucket!

All too soon it was time to leave the jovial company of the old Fish Inn, with many a backward glance as we picked up the waymarked track towards Broadway Tower. For somewhere within the vicinity of the little inn, which looked for all the world like an ornamental tea caddy in the distance, was where the Perry family of Campden was hanged in what must be the most mysterious of all unsolved mysteries.

Of all the confusing and conflicting accounts of what really happened to William Harrison, only the date of his disappearance is consistent. Thursday, 16 August 1660, the 70-year-old steward of Lady Juliana Noel set off to collect the Campden manorial rents. When he did not return, Mrs Harrison sent their servant John Perry to look for her husband. Perry told strange stories, each more bizarre than the other, of how Harrison had been robbed and murdered. After contradicting his evidence several times he accused his brother, Richard, and implicated his mother in the crime.

John Perry was committed for trial with his mother and brother at Gloucester Assizes, but the judge refused to try them as Harrison's body was not found. The following spring the Perry family were brought in front of Sir Robert Hyde, who disregarded proof of evidence and their protestations of innocence, and sentenced them to death. It was rumoured that Joan Perry was a witch so, in order to break the spell that she was supposed to have had on her two sons, she was hanged first. John ignored his brother's plea to tell the assembled crowd the truth and watched him die, too. Only when it was his turn to face the gallows did John Perry vehemently declare his innocence and promise that the truth would be revealed one day.

One day, two years after the Perry family had been executed for his supposed murder, William Harrison returned to Campden. The story he told to explain his disappearance was a weird and wonderful tale of how he had been kidnapped by Turkish agents and sold as a galley slave to Algerian pirates, capped by a whole catalogue of astonishing adventures in which he effected his escape and return to the Cotswolds. Harrison continued in the employment of Lady Juliana, whose idea it had been to have the Perrys executed on the hill as the most public place. Despite the glowing epitaph describing her as virtuous, the lady obviously had a strange streak of the macabre amongst her 'extraordinary great endowments' for she had her own memorial sculpted in her lifetime, ready to be revealed at her death. Just how much she was involved in this tragic miscarriage of justice will perhaps never be discovered in what has been locked into the legend of the Campden Wonder.

With such tales as travelling companions, it would be little wonder if the castellated round tower ahead did not suggest itself as something from Wonderland, appearing as it does like a gigantic chess piece on the skyline. Broadway Tower fulfils the 'dark Saxon' concept which James Wyatt planned for it. Apart from its ornate shape, the darkness of the North Country stone is in immediate contrast to the mellow honey-coloured Cotswold limestone. It amused me to see how the local stone had to be utilised for running repairs, the lighter blocks showing up like little patches on a schoolboy's trousers – a workaday touch on a rather austere and imposing edifice.

Follies of all shapes and sizes proliferated for all sorts of purposes in the eighteenth century. Broadway Tower was built by the Earl of Coventry in 1799 to satisfy, so tradition has it, a whim of his wife who, being so enchanted with the fact that a victory bonfire lit on Broadway beacon could be seen by the family at Croome Court, Worcester, requested that a tower be built as a landmark and reminder of the family's Springhill estate adjoining Broadway Tower. The earl sold both Springhill House and Broadway Tower around 1830, the former to General Lygon, the latter to Sir Thomas Phillips; Springhill had the attraction of a Capability Brown landscape, Broadway Tower, 'the broadest view in all England'.

The view from the 1,024ft (312m) hilltop is extensive; the view from the top of the tower, a further 55ft (17m) up, is panoramic. A record twelve counties can be seen from here – this was a baker's dozen before county planners drew new pencil lines along the old boundaries. Extending over 100 miles (160km) in each direction, on a clear day you can see from Shropshire's Wrekin in the north; beyond Bredon Hill, an outlier of the Cotswolds, and Evesham in its vale, to the Clee and the Clent and the Malverns; east to west from Border Hill of Leicestershire to the Black Mountains of Wales, and southwards to Cleeve Hill, the highest point on the Cotswold Way.

Broadway Tower is within the Broadway Tower Country Park, comprising country craft and natural-history exhibitions in the Tower and Rookery Barns, nature trails and picnic area, so to view from the top of the tower costs a fee; but the Cotswold Way route gives free passage through a hunting gate to skirt the tower. On through another gate and over four stiles to Rough Hill – quarryland dating back to monastic times from which the village of Broadway below was built in the pre-Reformation period. The hummocky grassland is a pincushion of wild flowers in spring and summer.

More stiles and a sunken track lead to a field then through a farmyard to complete the drop of some 500ft (152m) to the village. Looking back we can sympathise with William Morris who moaned about the steep climb to the tower with the picnic hamper while staying at Broadway with Burne-Jones and Rossetti.

# 2
# Broadway to Stanton

Busy, bustling, beautiful Broadway – its groups of gabled golden stone buildings appear on every Cotswold calendar, its name on every Cotswold tour. Broadway has attracted visitors over the ages; thriving from them, yet never succumbing to total commercialism. It trades like a town, but lives like a village.

From the tower walk, the route turns left affording a long walk through the village. Allow plenty of time to savour its delights even though the constant stream of traffic along its 'broad way' may irritate you after the quiet of the countryside. Without diverting for too long, it is worth the few steps to the right to see how sympathetic restoration has saved such lovely cottages as those flower-filled on Flea Bank, dating back to Shakespeare's time, and named after him. Three farms beyond have been home to an eminent politician, the Quaker Oats magnate and the aunt of the Queen Mother in their time, but are outstanding in their own right as well-preserved and improved farm buildings.

As with most villages that are on a long street plan, Broadway has its curved ends. Grampy Lewis used to say that village streets were designed that way to 'stop the folks at top end seeing what the folks at t'other end were up to', but, even without the curves, folks would have to be extraordinarily well-sighted to see the length of the High Street of 'Broddy' as the locals call it. In any case, there is much to attract comment along the way. Cotswold stone and Vale thatch marry happily on a roof-line pointed with gables and elegant chimneys, interspersed with low and long-slung ridges. Luxury hotels, business buildings, inviting inns and welcoming shops, historic houses and comely cottages stand shoulder to shoulder at all levels and of all ages in neat paving and grass and flower beds, some boldly beside the pavement, some edging shyly back in deeply recessed doorways. Almost immediately one is face to face with one of the oldest houses in Worcestershire – Prior's Manse, which properly echoes its monastic origins. Its near contemporary, The Grange, where the abbot lived, is beyond The Green at the far end of the village.

A44
BROADWAY
A44
Fish Hill
N
Very End
Church Street
A46
Broadway Coppice
St Eadburgh's Church
Broadway Tower
Snowshill
GLOS
WORCS
BUCKLAND
County Boundary
LAVERTON
Manor Farm
BROADWAY
TO
STANTON
No mans land
St Michael's Church
Mount Inn
STANTON
Guildhouse
Reservoir
Shenberrow Hillfort

Dog's Mercury

With the abbot at one end and his steward at the other, Broadway must have been well managed for the Benedictine monastery of Pershore to whom it belonged for some six hundred years.

Few of the many lovely buildings are without a snippet of history enclosed within their mellow walls and wrapped within their names. Milestone Hotel displays its milestone; the Lygon Arms displays its arms. A new slant on 'what the butler saw' is embodied in the story of this, one of Cotswold's most prestigious hotels.

*Cotswold stone and Vale thatch
in the High Street, Broadway*

In the early nineteenth century, General Lygon's butler was keeping an astute eye on the strategic position of the village in its increasingly important role servicing stage coaches on the London to Worcester run, while his lord and master was away commanding at Waterloo. The butler purchased the sixteenth-century White Hart Inn from the general and re-named it the Lygon Arms (pronounced Liggon), displaying his master's coat-of-arms in honour of his part in the victory, while the squire busied himself with planting his estate at Springhill with beeches emulating the formation of the troops drawn up in the great battle. The hotel was not only a viable venture, it survived the fluctuating fortunes which villages have always faced and, happily, it bred another success in the story of furniture making at Broadway.

Major extensions, renovations and refurbishing of the hotel at the turn of the century were carried out by the new owner's son, Gordon Russell – one of Chipping Campden's Ashbee school of craftsmen, influenced by William Morris to delight again in the sheer beauty of wood. Gordon Russell introduced to the North Cotswolds the craft of cabinet-making where no tradition of it existed before. The family business has outgrown its modest beginnings, but not its original concept – that simplicity of construction is the basis of good design. Marrying the traditional skills of cabinet-making to the technology of the twentieth century, means that furniture for church and schoolroom is available from the same workshops as furniture for Baghdad and Buckingham Palace. And what is nice is that this now world-famous firm sticks to its birthplace, behind the Lygon Arms, in Back Lane.

It was on a transient wintry-spring day that we set off from Broadway. The sun shone warmly on the winter-woolly clad shoppers and sightseers, burnishing the honey-coloured stone to a deep gold, with deep, cold shadows between the buildings and, as is the Cotswold way, we called on friends and fellow Wardens for a cup of tea; and where better to get to the heart of a village than at the newsagents? As usual, David Jelfs's attractive shop was busy, so we escaped to the flat roof over the back of the house and soaked up the early sun, watching the traffic crawling up long Fish Hill. The ridge of one of the two 400-year-old cottages – the last survivors of the many that once lined the street and now incorporated in the shop – had been newly thatched, and we traced our fingers over the scalloped edge of golden straw while Dave pointed out the datestone on the chimney of the house across the street, and chatted about the plans for the first guided walk along the Cotswold Way.

The sticky buds of the great chestnut trees were already fat, promising rich red blossom in the longer days ahead. We could afford but the briefest call at the Crown and Trumpet for a chat to old Gabriel, whose like has roamed the woods and wolds, hunting and hunted in the way of poachers, ever since the countryside's once-upon-a-time. Then to Collins's shop, proper pie-makers, who make the only original Gloucester sausage to the traditional recipe. The meaty, herb-speckled long sausage bears no resemblance to the bright-pink plastic rolls which pass under the same name. We joked about Gloucestershire's speciality being made in Worcestershire, but demand for it extends into south Wales, the Midlands and London's West End.

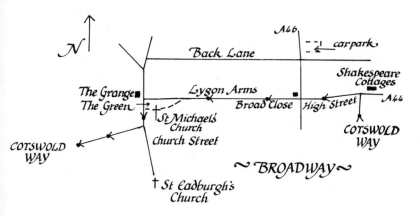

The route turns left at The Green and it is tempting to detour to the old church of St Eadburgh, which served the village for some seven hundred years before the Victorians decided it was too far away at the Very End and so built a new one by the village green. Just how much this decision was influenced by the resurrectionists' activities is not revealed, but body snatching was brisk business and up to £20 was paid for 'a good clean corpse' for dissection by many medical schools. Broadway was bedevilled by the repugnant trading, but the story takes on a bizarre twist in that the Reverend William Davies, the drunken parson, promised sure and certain resurrection – for it was his son who ensured it was! The gang was eventually caught and, since February 1831, the dear departed have rested in peace in this isolated spot.

The Cotswold Way leaves Broadway opposite the new church of St Michael by a hunting gate, then goes down a field and over a footbridge which spans the little Badsay Brook, blue with water forget-me-nots in summer. The series of stiles and fields is interrupted momentarily by West End Lane which cuts across to eventually join the A46 to Winchcombe. The hedge makes a good guide on this ascent to another hunting gate, the route then angles to Broadway Coppice. Every so often we had been stopping and looking back to get the feel of the Way walked from south to north, and we were glad we chose this point from which to do so, for the view of Broadway below is quite lovely. Recent rains had turned the woodland track to sticky clay mud, and we forecast what we could expect of the spring from the simple signs which countryfolk have observed throughout the ages – we decided the oak would be out before the ash, so we would only get a splash.

The walk through the wood ends at a gate, to continue along the hedgeline leading to farm buildings, and is well-marked. Gloucestershire is re-entered at the barns. A long farm track continues the ascent, affording a good view of Broadway Tower, and time to muse on how everything has a place and purpose in the 'great plan', because if the over-indulgent earl had not built such an eccentric property, the Royal Observer Corps would have been denied a ready-made observation post during World War II. And as we crossed No Man's Land over the cattle grid to follow the signs to Shenberrow Hillfort high up on the edge of the scarp, man's recent instinct to defend his homeland seemed not so far removed from that of those early Cotsallers who, in the Iron Age, used the liassic limestone for their spindle whorls and shaped the

local clay into pottery here on this wild wold. The hill-top valley
has a margin of scrubby thorn and gorse, and we foretold that
kissing would not be out of fashion yet for, between the tired
prickly spikes were a few golden sprigs.

The wooded track is quite steep as it leads to a field then sweeps
down to the reservoir, and so into Stanton by way of Sheppey
Corner. The sheep and shepherds of yesteryear no longer pass
this way to and from the rolling wolds above the village which
takes its name from 'stony farmstead'. Only the stone remains, to
be hewn from the heart of the land and fashioned with skill to
make a harmonious whole – Stanton is superb in its classic
simplicity of traditional Cotswold architecture.

But all is not old, and relegated to history; for a village becomes
a living heritage only when it has a continuity of culture and
character. This is illustrated by the Guildhouse, high up on the
rise to the right, beyond the Mount Inn. Here, in the quiet of the
Cotswolds where craftwork performs a particularly important
part in restoring human dignity and appreciation of life, Mary
Osborn set up a centre. Miss Osborn is a resolute idealist. The
story began when the children of the neighbouring hamlet of
Laverton used to visit her cottage, clutching fragments of fleece
caught on the wires and hedgerows and wanting to learn how to
spin it; and she dreamt of a place such as the Guildhouse where
country crafts and artistic skills could be brought to life again.

It was about fourteen years ago that I first visited the
Guildhouse. Mary Osborn had just realised her dream – the hall
was furnished with spinning wheels and the lichens and berries
and bark and flowers of the countryside overflowed from wicker
baskets, others had already yielded their soft and muted tones to
dye the wools. Everywhere was stone and wood, cut true to
delight the eye, the whole within a house built in the aristocratic
restrained style which marks the zenith of Cotswold domestic
architecture. Only the purity of the creamy stone singled it out as
newly built. I remember how I thought at the time that Cotswold
would, like the Corn King of old, come to life again, and how
bright and glowing our villages must have been when they were
newly built. Now those few years have mellowed the stone so that
it no longer stands out, but is woven into the tapestry of its softly
undulating landscape, testimony of a noble ideal in a community
of generous foresight and talent, built as it was of locally donated
materials and by voluntary and skilled craftsmen.

*Stanton*

Stanton wears its patina of age graciously, and commands instant respect. Even the post-war council houses are of traditional style and local stone. Nothing is obtrusive, apart from the ubiquitous motor car. Nevertheless, the clip-clopping of trotting horses is also a daily sound along the main street lined with lovely old houses, roofs angled steeply and mullioned windows set deeply. The day we were there, snowdrops demurely bowed their heads in the grass, displaying their pale green petticoats – a modest frivolity in the neat well-ordered scene.

Discretion is Stanton's distinction. We had passed the swimming-pool almost without noticing it at the top end and, had it not been for two lolly-licking tots emerging from a cottage-type doorway, we might have missed that near rarity – the village shop. The Stantons of Stanton see most of the Cotswold Way walkers, and judge whether they are just starting from the north or are on the home run from the south by the spring in the step or the shortening of the stride. They accept the restrictions about no signs outside their shop to advertise the service, but happily paper the spaces and timbers between the bottles and boxes and shelves with notices of village doings.

Stanton stands out in the memory as an experience. Few such villages remain so utterly unspoilt, thanks to the architect Sir Philip Stott who devoted his time, talent and resources to restoring it when he bought the estate in the Edwardian age. It is rather like walking through an old-master picture; for within the perfectly proportioned composition are many details of which to take measure. The oolitic stone hereabouts is richer in tone than that farther south along the scarp; shading from tawny gold to bronze it holds the sun on its face adding to the close-knit warmth of the homely grouping of manor and court, old farmhouses, medieval preaching cross and cottages all in a row. The timber-framed barns were evacuated here from elsewhere, but have blended well with their surroundings.

The village cross stands like a sentinel in the main street, its old base and shaft supporting a sundial, topped by a rounded finial and surmounted by a cross. John Wesley hitched his horse to a post and preached from its steps. The shepherds followed their masters to the even more ancient slender-spired St Michael's Church among the trees, and fastened their dogs to the poppy-head pew-ends; the deep gouges in the old wood tell the tale of many a fractious sheep-dog suffering many an over-long sermon.

The church itself is a delightful motley of all ages since Norman times. For centuries this humble village had shepherded vast flocks to swell the coffers of the great abbey in the valley; when Hailes fell in 1539, Stanton, like a prudent servant, salvaged a few treasures from its monastic master to enrich its own little church with a lovely stained-glass window. Young Stantonians who fell in World War I are commemorated in more modern glass, the wild strawberry in the window being the signature of Sir Ninian Comper who did much work refurbishing the churches of the Cotswolds. A 'rearrangement with open sittings' was undertaken in 1847 by Mr W. Bloxsome at his own expense, but he nevertheless offended the parishioners no end by taking down a singing gallery without their consent.

Large memorials in the church commemorate those who built the large houses, but to me the most memorable memorabilia were the homely handful of everyday stuff of everyday folk kept in the old muniments room above the porch. For in what must be the tiniest museum in the country a white cotton sunbonnet, a warming pan and well-worn pattens huddle together as in Gramp's musty old attic – eloquent echoes of summers past and winters long forgotten.

# 3
## Stanton to Hailes

The route leaves the main street, keeping left into Manorway and on to Chestnut Farm where a signpost shows the distances to Shenberrow Hill, Snowshill and Stanway. The sign to Stanway is clearly marked and follows the ridge and furrow shelf of the fields below the scarp slope and above the main road, over stiles and a footbridge. A tiny ball of emerald green moss was being laced with lichen by an industrious robin, while a water wagtail fussed among the vegetation alongside the shallow stream, discarding the wispy plumes of last year's willowherb for the downy fronds of the cat's-tail rush. The tread of our boots on the tangled roots sent a whole community of minute creatures scurrying and squittering, for all were astir at the feel of spring.

The Way descends diagonally across a fine avenue of trees and over two more stiles which, linked by trim iron railings, give an immediate impression of the old estate village. Across the road stands the cricket pavilion, a thatched timber building set up on the Cotswold staddle stones on which farmyard ricks were built. The most acrobatic rat would be defeated by these ingeniously shaped stone toadstools. Complete with two sides of cheerful cricketers, the pavilion looks for all the world like a carnival

*Stanway thatched cricket pavilion on Cotswold staddle stones*

N.

STANTON
TO
HAILES

St Michaels Church

Court

STANTON

Chestnut Farm

Cricket Pavilion

Tithe barn

B 4077

12th Century church of St Peter

Stanway House

DIDBROOK

WOOD STANWAY

Glebe Farm

Thrift Wood

Lower Goscombe

Stumps Cross

HAILES

Cromwell's Seat

Hayles Fruit Farm

Hailes Wood

Beckbury Camp

Campden Lane

Apple Blossom

FARMCOTE

St Faith's Church

float. It was a gift from Sir James Barrie who was a frequent visitor to Stanway House.

Stanway House just down the road is a splendid English Jacobean mansion, with a spectacular gatehouse fronting the main road. Burnished like old gold, the local stone is dramatically different from any other in the Cotswolds, and was fashioned

accordingly in an architectural extravaganza. Attributed to Inigo
Jones, it could just as easily be the design of one of the Strongs, a
Cotswold family of master masons whose works included
London's St Paul's. If the identity of the designer remains an
enigma, there is no such doubt as for whom the great house and
its remarkable gatehouse were designed, for etched against the
skyline are the scallop shells of the Tracy family.

Stanway House excites students of architecture by its wealth of
detail and they wax lyrical about Jacobean rustication, tran-
somed windows triple mullioned and Georgian entablature, but
the manor built on the site of the 'fair stone house' of the abbot of
Tewkesbury – in whose spiritual charge Stanway was for eight
hundred years – has also been home to some colourful characters
equally worthy of mention.

Sir William Tracy who obtained the Manor of Stanway from
the abbot of Tewkesbury in the strongly Catholic sixteenth
century was posthumously declared such a heretic, because of his
pointedly Protestant will, that the Archbishop of Canterbury had
his body exhumed and burnt at the stake. Nine years later,
Richard Tracy, Sir William's son, shattered the mystical magic
that was Hailes by taking the abbey's Holy Blood to London for
examination. Another Tracy quite contumeliously moved into the
west range of the old abbey whose downfall his forefather had
helped to engineer. The last Stanway Tracy married into the
Earls of Wemyss family in 1771. A claimant to a distant Tracy
peerage appeared on the scene in 1829 and caused the vicar of
Stanway to be summoned to the House of Lords together with the
parish registers dating back to 1656. In the event, the case for the
claimant, 'a middle-aged man with a strong Irish accent', was
declared fraudulent.

A completely different character from the politically powerful
Tracys was Dr Dover, said to be the grandson of the 'Cotswold
Olympicks' Robert Dover, and widely known as the 'Quicksilver
Doctor' from his introduction of mercury into medicine. He is also
accorded the fame of being the captain of the ship that rescued
Alexander Selkirk, on whose adventures Defoe based his classic
*Robinson Crusoe*. He was buried next door in 1742 in the little
church of St Peter, in the Tracy vault, although he was not
related to the family.

Remarkable for having changed hands only once in 1,260
years, other than by inheritance, Stanway House, in its quite

spectacular grounds next to the village church, is currently occupied by Lord and Lady Neidpath – he is son of the 12th Earl of Wemyss – who take great pride and pleasure in showing its treasures to the public on certain days in the summer months. They maintain that the interest of the house derives not from the national importance of its occupants, or its unknown architect, but from its development as a typical squire's manor house. It certainly embodies all the elements of the great house of the village. In the Great Hall the villagers of old assembled for the manorial court which was held here until about 1800; the Lord of the Manor would have sat on the raised dais meting out dues and the just deserts of the day, and the whole household would have taken their meals together under the 'coffered' panelled ceiling.

Delightful vignettes of domestic and administrative arrangements are portrayed in various rooms. The brewhouse was in use into living memory when a 'brewing woman' bicycled up to the great house each autumn to brew the barley crop. A separate little room was used specially for cleaning the many oil lamps which would have been in use until electricity was installed. Perhaps unique today is the audit room, for few, if any, estates still collects their rent by rent audit at which the tenants attend in person. Preservation of the special and precious visual harmony of the village is due entirely to the efforts and existence of Stanway Estate.

There is much else to attract attention inside the dwelling part of the house – the pair of unique 'Chinese Chippendale' day beds in the drawing-room, Brussels tapestries, other beautiful furniture and furnishings, the screens passage and minstrels' gallery.

Dark yews make a lovely background to the church, which is faced in the same golden ashlar as the great house. Inside, the

*Stanway House – the gatehouse and church*

over-zealous Victorians rather overdid its doing up, which has resulted in the most curious boundary wall on the north side of the churchyard. Fragments of carved masonry, 700 and 800 years old, and even stone coffins, obviously cleared out at this restoration, have been built into the stone wall and presented somewhat of a cultural shock to Nen and me, whose father laid miles of traditional dry-stone walls in his long lifetime. But it is well worth going round the churchyard to see because the carving is lovely and from there, too, is a superb glimpse of the great hall's west window, containing some sixty panes reaching almost to the eaves of the old house.

Behind the church is a magnificent tithe barn, with an expanse of stone-tiled roof supported by ancient cruck frames. It has been well cared for over the 600 years since it was built to store the abbot of Tewkesbury's dues. It now serves the village as an incredibly beautiful concert hall. The hand of Midas is everywhere in Stanway; nothing is commonplace but all is uncommonly elegant; and it is worth forsaking the green track for once in favour of following the road to the crossroads to see the exquisite bronze of St George and the Dragon – the village war memorial. Taking the left turn here on the B4077 will take you past, or tempt you into, the Old Bakehouse.

The route can be picked up again a few yards to the right at the head of Papermill Valley. Following the hedge-line, the hamlet of Wood Stanway is due south across the fields. Gnarled old apple trees were breaking into blossom around the farmhouses and cottages as we climbed the steep, gated, ridged and furrowed grasslands and on through Lower Goscombe Farm with many a pause to glance back and beyond for a superb view of Bredon Hill, an outlier in the lush green Vale of Evesham.

The rise of some 400ft (122m) emerges onto the B4077; turning right one needs to take great care here because of the blind bend on the hill. The beech-clad scarp summit is punctuated at Stumps Cross by an ancient stone stump – the remains of what was probably a wayside cross – hence its name, then the route veers right. A clutch of barns known as the Sheepwash, a shed perched on top of staddle stones and an old dewpond, are grouped as a timeless vignette of farming history. At Quarry Plantation the path angles north-west across to the hillfort at Beckbury Camp from which fine views are afforded of the surrounding countryside. Tradition seats the hated Thomas Cromwell at the north-west corner, a vantage point from which he watched Hailes Abbey burn. A monument at the spot is known locally as Cromwell's seat, but it could well have had more noble associations with the abbey itself; whatever the reason for its siting it was a splendid spot from which we marvelled at the vale below where great drifts of apple blossom merged into billowing clouds against the skyline. It was like looking suddenly ahead in time, for the fruit trees on the hills were markedly more hesitant to burst into flower.

Cotswold sheep on the skyline caught my eye as we followed the track across the fields. We called in on friends at Farmcote. The great house built stolidly into the scarp-line looked a different place in the spring sunshine from the elusive and mysterious manor which we had sought in the darkness of Twelfth Night. Then, in candlelight, we, together with our fellows of the Cotswold Sheep Society, had swapped stories over jugged hare and dreamt over our port of a spring day such as this with the lark high in the sky and leggy lambs in the grass. That day had come, and as we chatted with Maureen Vanderplank about the Cotswold Way over coffee on the lawn, Richard tended the last ewe to lamb and promptly christened the twins after us.

*Cotswold ewe and lamb*

The famed and fabled may have launched a thousand ships, but to be perpetuated by the noble Cotswolds on whose backs the whole history of our region developed, is a joy that can only be understood by such as we. Two more sheep means little in ordinary sheep terms, but in the fight for survival of this ancient and now rare breed, each one is significant. Elated by the prospect that the total world population of the Cotswold sheep had now reached a magnificent 400 (from a mere 20 at the turn of the century), we left the old house which had served the abbots of Hailes as their summer residence.

They, too, must have passed by the tiny yellow-stone rubble church of St Faith, for it was already old when Hailes was first founded. A brass vase of daffodils stood in a pool of golden light by the stone figures of the Stratford family, whose shield of arms is over the doorway of Great Farmcote manor house which we had just left. John Stratford was Lord Regent of England during the reign of Edward II, and succeeded to the office of Lord High Treasurer and Lord Chancellor; so he too, would have appreciated the value of the Vanderplanks' Cotswold twins.

We picked up the thread of our walk just below the cluster of medieval barns and farm buildings – a grange of the old abbey – to follow in the track of the old pilgrims. Ahead, the Malverns were a misty distant range beyond the Severn plain; then through the magic of a spring wood complete with a lovely wayfaring tree in the western corner, we dropped down to the vale and to historic Hailes.

# 4
# Hailes to Sudeley Castle

It was Easter when we met up again with Caroline, our producer. She sat awhile on a low stone wall of Hailes twelfth century church capturing the birdsong which filled the china blue sky. While she busied herself with the intricacies of sound recording, we introduced her little poodle, George, to the sights and scents of the countryside. George and a Jacob lamb eyed each other warily in the field beside the ruined abbey. George strained at his lead and bounced forward with an inquisitive bark for spotted lambs are fairly uncommon; the Jacob sprang to the safety of a clump of wild daffodils and gave a bewildered bleat, for chocolate coloured curly-coated dogs are even more uncommon in the Cotswold farmlands, as dogs are not encouraged in fields full of sheep.

*George and Jacob at Hailes*

Hailes Abbey is glorious in its ruin. It must have been magnificent in its prime. Nen spoke about its founding by Richard, Earl of Cornwall, on land given by his older brother, Henry III, as a thanksgiving for being saved from a shipwreck while returning from a crusade to the Holy Land. Hailes was one of the last abbeys founded for the Cistercians, and was dedicated in 1215 with great pomp – no fewer than thirteen bishops

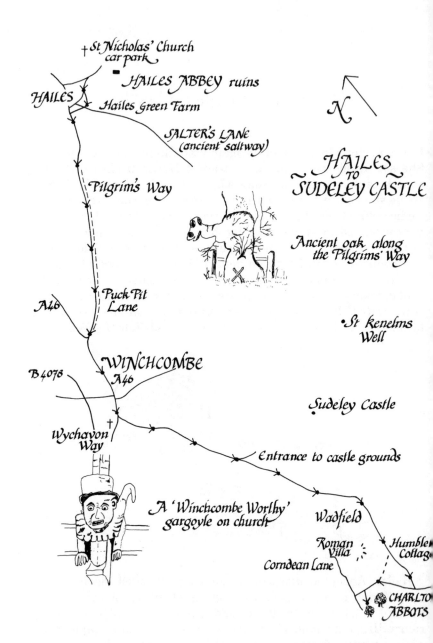

+ St Nicholas' Church
  car park
■ HAILES ABBEY ruins
HAILES    Hailes Green Farm
          SALTER'S LANE
          (ancient saltway)

N

HAILES
  TO
SUDELEY CASTLE

Pilgrim's Way

Ancient oak along
the Pilgrims' Way

Puck Pit
Lane

A46

· St kenelms
  Well

WINCHCOMBE
A46

B4078

Sudeley Castle

Wychavon
Way

Entrance to castle grounds

A 'Winchcombe Worthy'
gargoyle on church

Wadfield

Roman
Villa

Humble
Cottage

Corndean Lane

CHARLTON
ABBOTS

attended the ceremony in company with the king and Eleanor his queen. The Cistercian Order was a branch of the Benedictines, and the fertile plain was conducive to the farming to which their lifestyle was committed, the manual toil leavened only by daily prayer.

It was Richard's son Edmund who presented the abbey with its most precious asset. Just how the phial of Holy Blood was obtained, completely authenticated by Pope Urban IV as being the blood of Christ, is open to scholarly squabble, but the fame and prosperity it brought to the abbey is beyond dispute. To house it, the east end was rebuilt with an elaborate arrangement of chapels as in a coronet, the crowning jewel being the holy relic. A later gift, also from Edmund, was a gold cross in whose enamel base was embodied a splinter of the True Cross, but it was the Holy Blood which attracted pilgrims from far and wide to seek out this rural spot and absolution. Only when they had contributed heartily to the coffers were the penitent pilgrims allowed a glimpse of the holy relic immortalised by Chaucer in the *Pardoner's Tale* as 'By the Blode of Crist that is in Hayles'. However, an examination of it before king and council revealed it to be either the blood of a duck or 'honey clarified and coloured with saffron' – a dupe not easily forgiven by Henry VIII who had himself made a pilgrimage to what was by then one of the greatest, and certainly one of the wealthiest, of the country's thousand monasteries.

*Hailes Abbey ruins*

Political and personal avarice marked out Hailes for dissolution rather than its fall from grace, and the abbey was surrendered on Christmas Eve 1539. Stripped of its plate and possessions, and plundered for its stone, the remains of church and chapter house, chapels and cloister were ravaged and plundered for four hundred years until the then Ministry of Works took it over. Extensive excavations exposed the foundations, and restoration cleaned the ancient arcades of grime and ivy, so that the ground plan and the little that remains of the arched walls are now pristinely preserved and afford an idea of the immensity of the buildings. Relics and reconstructions, and superbly sculpted stone in the adjoining museum, exhibit the splendour that once was Hailes.

The little church opposite, secluded by an old yew speckled with starlings, is scarcely the size of a barn. It must have appeared but a humble cell in the shadow of the great abbey, but what it lacks in proportion it makes up for in antiquity. Built about 1130, it had long served an old-established local community before the Cistercians possessed it; but it bears witness to its allegiance to the founder of the abbey in the arms and heraldic devices of its wall-paintings and tiles. Saints and sporting scenes, monks and mythical monsters painted by some medieval hand and delightfully jumbled up, enliven the walls. It is well cared for by the tiny dedicated community; but today's polish and detergent has little effect on the magic that only eight and a half centuries can impart to such a place. It is a little church with great charm.

The route to Winchcombe is boldly signposted opposite the car park which is conveniently sited by the church, but built to serve the visitors to the abbey ruins. The hunting gate made a singing swinging sound as we passed through into the field. Banks of primroses spilled drops of pale yellow light into the dark brook, thickly vegetated, the trickle of water running through the gulley now but an echo of the *Haylebrok* – the stream which gave the site its name. The field is crossed at an angle and one can look back again at the arches of the ancient abbey. However tumultuous were its times and violent its end, the tranquillity of its setting is inviolate; all is at pastoral peace in the protection of the Historic Buildings and Monuments Commission.

A gate leads to a stony track alongside Hailes Green Farm, built largely, no doubt, from stones from its reverend neighbour. A barn was being converted into a house and we got a cheery

wave from the masons juggling with stone quoins. As we turned
right on to Salter's Lane – the tail-end of the ancient track along
which the medieval salt carriers and their packhorses trudged
from Droitwich to serve the monasteries, manors and merchants
across the Cotswolds – a light breeze wafted a tantalisingly sweet
perfume, the distinctive scent of balsam poplars breaking bud in
a spring-sunlit lane.

The route turns left to climb a rough track. White-blossomed
blackthorn made delicate lace patterns in the new green of the
hedgerow. A little further on, target waymarks, like countryside
'lollipop ladies', direct foot-traffic diagonally across a cultivated
field. A chuttering tractor breasting the swell of a neighbouring
field, followed by a score of noisy seagulls, proved too strong an
opposition for my recording describing the kissing gate – of
country cunning to keep courting couples in and cattle out.
Caroline recounted some of the stories behind the stories which
she had covered on outside broadcasts. How Chaucer would have
loved The Producer's Tale of following a great churchman's
progress through the kingdom – a parody suggested by the fact
that we were actually walking along the Pilgrims' Way, with the
glimpse of an occasional slab of the original paving punctuating
the point. The centuries telescoped to a timelessness of travellers
walking and talking together.

The medieval pilgrims did not benefit from the voluntary work
of the Cotswold Wardens as modern walkers do – an excellent
example of the latter's work being the building of the rather
splendid footbridge and as important, although not so aestheti-
cally apparent, the improved surface of the approach to Puck Pit
Lane. In Old English the name means 'goblin-haunted hollows';

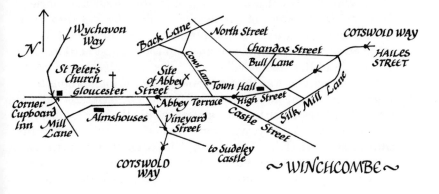

there is certainly a magical air about any country lane in springtime, and in Puck Pit this is especially so. Particularly late-flowering catkins, 'lamb-tails' as we call them, shook their soft pollen in the stiffening breeze, covering the scarlet tufts of the female flowers with crusty golden dust – just nature's way of propagation by airmail. It is incredible that each catkin has nearly four million grains of pollen. Most of it falls on barren ground, of course; but an old country saying 'a good nutting year means a good baby year' may have derived from a wise old sage knowing as much about the love-life of the hazel as do erudite ecologists. Blackthorn was there to foretell a cold spell and a plentiful harvest of purple sloes for autumn; oak and ash and sycamore stood boldly above the thick quickthorn; dark-eyed violets peeped from the cover of the uncurling leaves of lords-and-ladies, and Jack-by-the-hedge spiced the air with its garlic smell as I crushed it underfoot while looking for the delicate wind-flower, or Easter wood anemone. A small millstone built into a dry-stone wall had been put to ingenious use to channel water from a tiny brook through the hole to cascade into a ditch running alongside the lane. We were soon overtaken by quick-striding walkers when scudding white clouds dropped their showers, but the sun and the glossy golden celandines were out again by the time we had reached the houses coming up the lane to meet us.

Turn left onto the busy A46 to enter Winchcombe. The path passes over the Isbourne at Footbridge; a qualm of disorientation is experienced here because your map and instincts tell you that you are heading south, yet the river is flowing north. It does so for its entire length and must be one of very few to do so in the British Isles.

The Way follows the main road into the small and ancient town, still in the steps of the medieval pilgrims, and they were but following an already well-beaten track for the *wincel* (bend) in the *combe* (valley) had been home to the earliest settlers. The Neolithic and Roman Cotsallers preferred the higher ground up on the scarp face; it was the Saxons who laid the foundations from which Winchcombe developed into a town of considerable fame – in fact, loyal locals mutter over a glass darkly that here, albeit for a brief period in history, was the capital of all England. Records substantiate the claim it has as having been capital of its own county, although Winchcombshire lasted but from 1007 to 1017 and was then swallowed up in the administrative shire of the city of Gloucester. But it was a royal seat. Offa, King of Mercia, founded a nunnery here in 789, and his successor, King Kenulf, founded the abbey in 811.

Street names perpetuate the many and varied aspects of the town's history, and as one follows Hailes Street's windings up towards the High Street, a visit to the small museum in the Victorian Town Hall built in Tudor style puts some of it into chronological order. Its exhibits range from bones from Belas Knap Long Barrow to tanners' tools and bits of the old silk-mill machinery. It is also the International Police Museum. The fearsome wooden stocks are preserved outside, under a neat stone-tiled roof – a nicety denied to those unfortunate enough to have been clamped and cramped into them. The seven-holes design is unique in the Cotswolds and was built to accommodate the local one-legged trouble-maker who always managed to get himself 'stocked-up' with other felons (at least, that is what the cheerful curator told me!)

The stocks, Winchcombe

The George Inn opposite, with its galleried courtyard, was built as a hostel for pilgrims attracted to Hailes, but much earlier they came to the great Benedictine abbey in Winchcombe itself, north-east of the parish church. The abbey was important, powerful and possessive. It was one of the largest of the ecclesiastical landowners of the Middle Ages, and had control of all but two of the churches in the parishes where it held land. The legend of Saint Kenelm was what brought pilgrims from far and wide to pay dues and homage to this shrine where diverse miracles were reputedly worked. The story of the boy king, son of the abbey's founder, was known to Chaucer, but is of such dramatic consequence that it could belong more readily to some ancient Greek tragedy. Logic will never unlock long-loved folklore so it is useless to question the improbable behaviour of the bird and beast in the fable. In any case it is a moral tale and has stood the test of time.

King Kenelm – varied versions age him anything between seven and twenty years old – was taken hunting by Ascobert, his tutor and his sister's lover. The sister, Quendreda, who was jealous of her brother's accession, arranged to have him killed, and Ascobert carried out the dastardly deed while the young Kenelm was chanting 'Te Deum' in the Clent Hills forest. As the boy was beheaded, a white dove flew off to Rome and dropped a scroll on the High Altar as the Pope was celebrating Mass. On it was the message:

> In Clent cow-pasture under a thorn
> of head bereft lies Kenelm, king-born.

Kenelm's pet white cow led the monks to where her master's decapitated body was buried. On its long procession back to Winchcombe, springs gushed forth wherever the body was rested; the one on Sudeley Hill was commemorated by the building of a chapel on the site. The original chapel was demolished in Victorian times, but the spring was put to good use by the philanthropic Emma Dent of Sudeley Castle to provide water to the town to mark Queen Victoria's Golden Jubilee. A small statue and a reference on the OS maps mark the well.

The young king was later canonised, but retribution was swift on the wicked sister for legend has it that, as she was attracted to the window of Kenulf's palace (where Lloyds Bank now stands) by the chanting of the monks and peered down on the brother whose murder she had designed, she was struck blind. Records speak of penitent Quendreda becoming abbess of Southminster nunnery in Essex. Excavations in 1815 of Winchcombe abbey revealed two stone coffins, in one of which was the remains of a child – and a knife. The coffins are to be seen in the parish church.

Of the abbey, nothing remains. It was surrendered on the same cold and windy night as Hailes tolled its great bell for the last time; a single cross marks the spot where its High Altar stood, now on private ground behind a high wall. But the ghosts of seven hundred monastic years are never still: a murmured litany lingers on a gentle breeze in the trees overhanging the wide pavements, and the abbey's rich past lives on in name and fame.

Winchcombe's early abbots were blessed with such shrewd business acumen that, by investing the offerings from pilgrims to St Kenelm's shrine, the abbey flocks grazed for a dozen miles on manor ground which the abbots owned on the Cotswold hills above. One free landholder, John le Kayt who lived some 5 miles (8km) away at Hawling, was persuaded over the years to part with his land portion by portion, often 'for the good of his soul', sometimes for a sum 'for his great necessity' and finally for board, lodging and necessities of clothing. The small village of Charlton Abbots, where the monks founded a leper hospital, originated as a farmstead of the peasants (*ceorl tun*) belonging to the abbots.

A fifteenth-century merchant from Florence listed Winchcombe as twelfth in order of monastic wool production, estimating somewhat conservatively that its 8,000 sheep were bringing in an annual income of around £400. Across its vast sheepwalks ran the arteries of medieval commerce – the prehistoric way running south-west to the port of Bristol, the Roman Fosseway linking the southwest to and beyond the Midlands, and the Salt Way to the navigable upper reaches of the Thames at Lechlade. Yet despite these advantages, Winchcombe never developed as a wool centre in the same way as other Cotswold market towns.

The division between monastic and civic life was deep seated and long lasting. Abbey and town co-existed on ambivalent terms – the town's trade centred on accommodating the pilgrims, but as the abbey owned most of the property it clawed back in rents a considerable percentage of the income. The townsfolk protested, some violently, by physically attacking the monks after breaking into the monastery and stealing precious plate. Successive vicars were equally vociferous, and used the church bells' iron tongues to speak for them so loudly during meditation that it took a papal decree to stop the provocative peals. It has been hinted that the grotesque gargoyles on the church were caricatures of some of the most hated of the monks; locally, they are known as the 'Winchcombe Worthies' – but worthy of, or for what, is left to conjecture. Under its penultimate abbot, Richard Kidderminster, the abbey became an academic seat 'equal to a little University', and he achieved national fame by being the king's ambassador to Rome. Intellectual and influential, he found favour with Henry VIII and friendship and patronage from Thomas Cromwell, neither of whom spared the abbey from dissolution. Kidder-minster died in 1531, so was spared seeing the destruction of the monastery he had served for fifty-six years.

Unshackled at last from its monastic master, the town picked the abbey's stones; but building a new fabric for its economy was more difficult, since the great medieval wool trade had already declined. What it did salvage was on an individual rather than communal scale. Only four mercers were recorded in the early seventeenth century; and it is for botany rather than wool cloth that the name of one of them is remembered. Christopher Merrett, who lived in what was the old Crown Inn by Mill Lane, in 1666 published his *Pinax* – a catalogue of flora, fauna and minerals including the first recorded list of British birds. The first edition suffered extensive damage in the Great Fire of London, but was reprinted the following year. Merrett, educated at Oxford, became a physician of note and librarian to the Royal College of Physicians, but he is remembered for his contribution to British botany rather than his not insignificant one to medicine. A group of algae was accorded the name *Merrettia* in his honour. Of the wild peony, descended from the hoary legends of the Trojan Wars where it healed Pluto and other wounded gods and, more locally, seeded from the monasteries' herb gardens, no trace has been found despite the diligent searches of successive botanists.

One of the few successful clothiers was Jack Smallwood, who manufactured Winchcombe jerseys but became better known as Jack o' Newbury who financed a force of some 300 men to fight at Flodden Field in 1513. Battle royal waged on Winchcombe's own doorstep during the Civil War, but it was Sudeley Castle which suffered the most structural damage; the town itself was regarded as but poor and beggarly according to contemporary chronicles.

Parliamentary troops under a later monarch were again dispatched to the quiet little town, this time as Pepys recorded: 'to spoil the tobacco there, which the people do plant contrary to law and always have done'. There is a long-cherished belief that Raleigh planted the first seeds; the tradition far outlived the trade, however, for strong opposition from West Indian and Bristol merchants forced the government to pass an Act pro-hibiting tobacco planting. But having at last founded a profitable trade, the tobacco farmers flouted the law for as long as they could and 'daily took it to London by secret ways'. Now Winchcombe baccy, like old Jack's jerseys, is but history, but explains the name Tobacco Close for a small housing estate which we passed on the edge of the town. A short-lived silk-throwing industry made use of an old fulling mill and young child labour, but a paper mill downstream at Postlip has survived and still meets the demands of a modern age.

*The Old Corner Cupboard,*
*Winchcombe*

We normally call in at the Old Corner Cupboard for a bar snack, and I strain my ears for the pitter-patter of the little girl ghost's footsteps; but, as Jean and Michael Elliott say, there are many creaks and squeaks and bumps in the night in a house over 400 years old. The lovely old inn, with its heavy studded oak door under a Tudor arch, was a farmhouse until about 1850. As was the custom at the time, the inn gave away clay pipes with every purchase of tobacco, and when the Customs and Excise men visited to say that the pipes should be stamped to identify the inn from which they were given, the landlord hastily named it from the extraordinary number of corner cupboards in the place; today, there are only two. This time we forsook the hospitality of the old hostelry for home-made cheese scones filled with Double Glou-cester made by George Martell, the only traditional Gloucester-shire cheese-maker.

The route leaves Winchcombe by way of tree- and terrace-cottage lined Vineyard Street, signposted 'Sudeley Castle'. The Isbourne, at the end of Vineyard Street, was where the town scolds and witches received their rough and wet treatment on their duckboard stool. Downstream, its waters with the special properties associated with rare north-flowing rivers are still put to use at the old-established paper mill.

The castle lodge entrance is pretty with castellated archway and tower, and not yet a century old. The Sudeley Estate, like Winchcombe, was important before the Conquest; but it was not until the authorities were engaged in the warring wrangles of Stephen and Matilda that a castle was built – apparently illegally. The earliest features of the rebuilding in the fifteenth century by Ralph Botelar, Baron of Sudeley and Lord Chamberlain, are the outer and inner courts on the north and south respectively, with the church of St Mary and the great barn on the east and west ranges.

Sudeley Castle

The castle was a prized piece on the royal chessboard. Edward IV confiscated it, because Botelar supported the Lancastrians in the Wars of the Roses; later it was held by Richard III. The Tudors retained it as a royal seat and Henry VIII stayed there with Katherine of Aragon and, later, with Anne Boleyn. But it was with his widow, Katherine Parr, that the castle is most strongly associated, for in 1547 she married Lord Seymour who had been given the property that very year. Katherine Parr died in 1548, a few days after giving birth to a daughter. The fate of the little Mary Seymour remains a mystery, but if historians paid scant attention to her, the diehards did not let the controversial Katherine rest in peace. Her funeral service, conducted in English, was radical for the day and regarded as provocatively Protestant. The appointment of Miles Coverdale as almoner was proof of the scholarly queen's intense interest in progressive religious theories, for Coverdale was continuing the work started by William Tyndale, who features further south on our walk.

Sequestrated on Seymour's death, Sudeley was granted to Lord Chandos who held it for the king. Charles I stayed there following the raising of the siege of Gloucester, but it fell to Cromwell's army who desecrated Katherine Parr's tomb and violated the body. Chandos changed sides and paid his fines, but the castle was 'slighted' and left pretty well uninhabitable for some 200 years, although George III did 'call to see' – but fell down a staircase so did not stop!

What is seen of Sudeley today is what was rescued and restored by the Dents, a glove-magnate family and benefactors of Winchcombe generally. Visitors respect that it is a stately home which is still home to the family who have done so much to present its past in such a way as to safeguard its future. They come to see the ruins of the great banqueting hall, Europe's largest collection of children's toys, the Old Masters and tapestries and the lovely old castle itself, where many historical dramas have been filmed so that the splendours of Sudeley have been transmitted to millions through the eyes of television cameras.

# 5
# Sudeley Castle to Cleeve Common

Just past the entrance to Sudeley Castle, a signpost on the right points the way to Belas Knap, and the route strikes diagonally across ridge and furrow, over stiles, fields and footbridges and alongside thorny hedge-edged farmland for a mile (1.6km) to Wadfield. The name is a corruption of 'woad', which was once planted to supply the dyers in the woollen industry. Licensing the growing of woad was one of the monopoly rights Elizabeth I granted for raising revenue; a rent of around £17 was payable on each 100 acres planted. Families migrated to the woad fields for harvesting in much the same way as their south-east contemporaries did for hop-picking. The plant, used in Roman Britain, is said to have given a similar blue to the rarer indigo after oxydising in the air; the earliest Anglo-Saxon record of the then native woad was in 342. It is now difficult to find enough plants growing wild to justify picking them for home dyeing. Wadfield farmhouse, built about 1700, is unusually fine in proportion and style, and may well reflect the one-time value of the woad fields. The path goes round the house on the left-hand side.

On the ascent to Humblebee Cottage, a partially excavated Roman villa hides among the fir trees to the right. A shed gives some protection to a restored and re-sited mosaic floor. Ask at Humblebee Cottage for access.

As we turned right onto the country lane which runs from Charlton Abbots at the tip of Breakheart Plantation, a following of long-legged lambs bounced up and down bleating most vociferously as though questioning why anyone should want to leave a lush hillside for a metalled road; but this one is narrow and cuts across the steep bank and is hung all about with budding beech and crab apple. An important pointer shows that the route veers left to climb a little way through the wood where last autumn's leaves shelter this spring's primroses. The delicate lilac cuckoo-flowers, or lady's smock, nodded from the damp ruts; and dog's mercury, which we had first noticed in early February, was still with us. We initiated a small group of foreign visitors in the

Bishop's Cleeve

A46

N↑

Corndean Lane

Cleeve Hill Youth Hostel

The Ring ▲ 1040 ft

Castle Rock
CLEEVE COMMON

Thrift Wood

Hillfort

Huddlestone's Table

Queens Wood

Knoll Hill Farm

Happy Valley

Radio masts

▲ 1083

SUDELEY CASTLE TO CLEEVE COMMON

Wood Anemone

Evans Adlard paper mill

+ St James's Church

• Postlip Hall

Breakheart Plantation

Corndean Hall ■

Charlton Abbots

Humblebee How

Hill Barn

Hill Barn Lane

BELAS KNAP Long Barrow

Wontley Farm

Belas knap false portal

intricacies of getting through the kissing gate at the top – without involving ourselves in the implications of its name. The protruding knotty roots of an ancient beech tree made a series of natural steps to the field where early green shoots pierced the rich red Cotswold soil. As we skirted the edge of the field, and paused for breath as the climb is long rather than steep, I looked back to envisage the Way walked south to north, and tried to describe in my recording the view of Sudeley nestling like a golden fairy-tale castle in the valley below, with Winchcombe embayed in its broad but cosy combe. Over all, swiftly shifting cloud shadows played tag with sunlit fields and jumbled up the Georgian enclosure pattern of the landscape.

The ragstone used for the boundary wall here is of the older and thinner Inferior Oolite, and as we edged along the top of Humblebee How and reached Belas Knap (pronounced locally as Bellasnap) it was the construction of the stone walling that delighted me. Here the Neolithic folk had quarried the stones and laid them one on another in exactly the same way as father did, and generations of wallers before him, to stretch for miles like a great chunky necklace across the bosom of Mother Cotswold. Excitedly, I pointed out to Caroline that there was not 'a Bristol join' in sight – a waller's derogatory term for a stone on top of another so placed as to make a straight line of the edges. 'One over two, and two over one' was Pop's way of describing how to build a weatherproof dry-stone wall. The durability of the building method is evidenced in the revetment walls, for they have withstood some five thousand winters. The stone is very regular in shape and thin enough to resemble Cotswold 'slats', sometimes called Stonesfield slates – a misleading term really as they are not geological slate but fissile limestone which, after quarrying, is left out for the frost to split into layers for tiling.

Belas Knap is the finest example in the county of the Severn-Cotswold series of false-entrance type Neolithic long barrows. Time has moulded the complex arrangement of burial chambers, linked by passages and roofed with stone slabs, into a huge grass-covered mound supported by some 180yd (165m) of dry-stone wall, 13ft (4m) high. An original extra revetment wall was dismantled and the stones rebuilt to enclose the barrow. The false portal consists of a large stone slab between two horns, behind which an exploration of 1863 revealed a forecourt with the skull of a round-headed young man, possibly of the Beaker people, and the remains of five children. Inner chambers contained long-headed skulls. The attempts to defeat tomb pirates by building a false portal did not succeed entirely, for when the barrow was explored in Victorian times, then excavated and restored in the 1930s, it was evident that the Romans had already burrowed into the barrow so the artefacts are meagre and mainly Romano-British.

In its utter simplicity and primeval purpose, Belas Knap is hauntingly majestic. Against the sheltering shoulder of Humble-bee How woodland, the mystery of a million seasons is entombed and stands as its name suggests like a beacon on the hilltop – as alone as Adam. The route passes in front of the north-facing portal across an arable plateau. The old saying 'as slow a-coming as Cotswold barley' is well understood on these wind-swept uplands. At Hill Barn Lane bear left south-westward to pass Wontley Farm. It is significant that the stone wall, the most prominent feature of the enclosures' effect on the physical pattern of the Cotswold landscape, terminates at the point where it meets common land.

# 6
# Cleeve Common to
# Dowdeswell Reservoir

The Way takes on a quite different character here on Cotswold's last unenclosed commonland. For some 5 miles (8km) it takes a sinuous track to skirt the massive syncline which makes Cleeve Common a place for all people for all reasons. Covering some 3sq miles (7.8km$^2$), it is by far the largest Common on the Cotswolds; it is also the highest point. It may only reach to the midriff of a mountain, but at 1,083ft (330m) it is the highest area in lowland England east of the River Severn, and at some 180 million years of age it must rank as one of the oldest. The earliest Iron Age people fortified the westerly edge and the Romans left miniature bronze votive objects including a ploughshare and a sword in honour of Mars, their god of agriculture, and large triangular clay loom weights as evidence of their wool industry.

The waymarking is extensive and leads off northward, but to visit the highest point take the left-hand path on entering the Common and make for the trig point south-east of the radio masts on West Down. Dawn walkers may well encounter early morning jockeys crouched over their cantering mounts on the gallops beyond the gorse across the broad plateau on the west. Winding its way across Padcombe Valley where the Isbourne rises, the route assumes more of a moorland character; but while heather and tussock and close-cropped turf clothe the steep slopes and dry valleys there is an abundance of those flowering plants that flourish on limestone: Cotswold penny-cress, kidney vetch, basil thyme, woolly thistle, pasque flower, milkwort, rock-rose and squinancywort – names that trip off the tongue like ancient charms.

About a mile (1.6km) up the common, a curiously shaped sheepdip below the dam looks like a giant keyhole. The key to the secret ways of the Washpool Valley belongs to the walker. At the head of Postlip valley a group of gabled Jacobean hall, Tudor tithe barn and Norman chapel stands in glorious tree-shaded

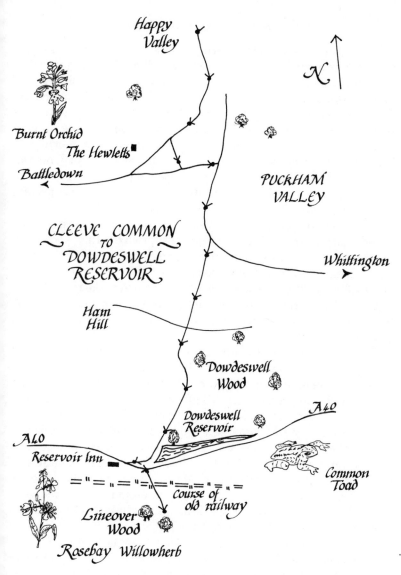

Happy Valley

N

Burnt Orchid

The Hewletts

Battledown

PUCKHAM VALLEY

CLEEVE COMMON
TO
DOWDESWELL
RESERVOIR

Whittington

Ham Hill

Dowdeswell Wood

A40

Dowdeswell Reservoir

A40

Reservoir Inn

Common Toad

= " = " = " = " = " = " =
Course of old railway

Lineover Wood

Rosebay Willowherb

seclusion. An enchanting enclave, Postlip is now owned by a housing association, its families all keen to preserve its aura of history and conserve its natural environs. Built originally on wool-trade profits, the mellowed old mansion in the 1860s housed the Evans Adlard family who owned the paper mill deeper down the valley, the bailiff, carter and shepherd sharing the great house with their master and the grain and mangold stocks.

The cathedral-like tithe barn is said to have been used for drying Winchcombe's tobacco harvest. The little effigy on the western gable, like all ancient and curious Cotswold stones, comes down at midnight to drink – Sir William de Postlip favours Queen Bess's Well below the bank in front of the hall! St James's is thought to be the oldest Roman Catholic chapel in the country and was built about 1144 to save Postlipians the journey to Winchcombe. It is now annexed to Winchcombe parish. The hall and grounds are sometimes open for special events; the entrance is off the A46 Winchcombe road but, on occasion, the private 'Ben's gate' onto Cleeve Common is opened.

It is safer to respect the waymarked route close to the gorse-edged margin and off the golf-course fairways. Just above the club house, the Way loops left to descend the west side of the spur, undulating over ancient quarried slopes to The Ring. There is an almost Hobbit-like mystique about this Iron Age earthworks – a verdant vortex tantalizing our imagination of a lost people. A track to the western edge leads to the only youth hostel on the Cotswold Way.

The views across to the outlier hills – Bredon, Dumbleton and Langley – are a tempting introduction to those to be encountered along this open, almost wild, stretch of country. Castle Rock on the left is an impressive sheer cliff of Lower Freestone, usually hung about with intrepid rock climbers, while their timorous fellows above fly kites on the skyline and school parties below pick at the Pea Grit. Cleeve is a geologist's paradise and schools from far and wide hoard chunks of its fossiliferous foundations in their classroom cupboards. Botanists busy themselves looking for bee, purple, burnt-tip and green-winged orchids, while we were thrilled to spot glow-worms sparking off bright pin-points of light among the tiny shell fragments where they had been feeding in the shady edge alongside Thrift Wood. A small herd of lively heifers stampeded down the hill, scattering loose stones in their wake; but as we neared the end of the tree-shaded track under Cleeve Cloud a flock of fleet-footed sheep passed us in orderly fashion, restoring the pastoral peace. A drinking trough built into the hillside is another reminder that this is common grazing land.

Waymarking appears on boulders, but many tracks traverse the Common to tempt the walker to higher vantage points to pick out May Hill and the Malverns and the Black Mountains in the panoramic patchwork stretching away to a hazy horizon. Such a view under sun-edged thunder clouds is spectacular, but it is a bleak place to be at the wrong end of a storm; on the high gallops stable lads know better than any how winter rains can freeze as they fall on the face. On the lower, parallel, track, harebells and humpy hummocks encircle Huddlestone's Table, under the sloping shadow of the Iron Age hillfort. The Huddlestone family were granted common rights some four hundred years ago, but tradition has it that the stone was already ancient and marks the spot where King Kenulf bad farewell to the notable guests who had witnessed the dedication of his abbey at Winchcombe. We made use of the curious cuboid stone table for our picnic.

*Huddlestone's table, Cleeve Hill*

A lone dog howled somewhere beyond Queen's Wood and filled the sweeping vale with its plaintive cry. It was such a contrast to the spring day a decade ago when we were surveying and waymarking the Cotswold Way. Then the great skein of Prestbury Racecourse below was shimmering with the silks chasing round for the coveted Cheltenham Gold Cup, the swell and fall of the crowd's animation rising up to us on the escarpment. Home of the National Hunt Festival, Prestbury Park has a special place in racing annals, and over 3,000 soldiers from World War I had good reason to remember it with some affection when the grandstand, ladies' drawing room and luncheon rooms were turned into a Red Cross hospital. Race meetings were still held and for five years, as was reported in *Town Topics*, 'it was khaki, khaki everywhere, and long rows of wounded men with their nurses watched the racing from the Stands'. Some of the soldiers even rode in the steeplechase, and one Belgian was said by *The Sporting Times* to have, despite his wounds, jumped 'some of the biggest fences on the course on foot'. Like the lone trees holding each other up on the breezy upland, the ghosts of Black Tom and the legendary Fred Archer – who, as a plaque on the Kings Arms Inn, his old home, at Prestbury purports, 'trained upon toast, Cheltenham water and toffee' – ride the rough winds on the Cleeve gallops, alongside which is the alternative trod to the end of the Common, marked by a massive noticeboard.

There is a wall on the right side of the path, radio masts on the left. Gates and waymarks skirt the beech wood to head due south and down the dry lateral dip with the lovely name of Happy Valley, inhabited only by tiny creatures of the countryside. You are still on a Site of Special Scientific Interest, designated by the Nature Conservancy Council as Grade 1. Over the stile the Way drops through thick gorse scrub, but the path is well cleared. The incursion of modern motor-bike mania often rends the rural solitude here, at the old quarry. A gate leads to a stony track and another gate takes you alongside a narrow woodland to join a minor road which goes to Whittington. Between The Hewletts and Puckham Valley, on the then only road from the east into Cheltenham, the Earl of Essex with some 15,000 soldiers marched on to relieve Gloucester in 1643, and camped for two rainy days hereabouts along the Cotswold Way. At a gate on the right the Way leaves the road and runs alongside a field, another gate takes you down to cross over a stile at each side of Ham Hill by road. Target waymarks direct trampling boots safely across a cultivated field.

It was early evening when we left the sun-lit wolds under sizzling pylon wires. To the south-east the pattern of fields fell away and over to Andoversford. The approach to Dowdeswell Wood is deceptive, a stile between low bushes of elder and hazel gives no clue as to the dense and tangled woodland through which you drop some 300ft (91m) for almost a mile (1.6km). Dog's mercury was still thick underfoot, with the flora of the woods – violet, anemone, spurge and sorrel, attracting our constant attention. Bluebells massed in dark, deep scented dells and homing birds warned of our passing. The path follows the westerly edge of the wood and it is particularly lovely with the sinking sun shafting through the tall trees, stopping short at the foot of the plantation densely packed with Scots pine, cypress,

*Sheered slope in Dowdeswell Wood*

larch, spruce and poplar and separated from the old ash, oak, hazel, beech and wych elm by a high wire fence. Fellow Cotswold Wardens had recently sheered the steepest gradient into planked steps, a tremendous improvement on the hitherto slippery slope.

A rustle behind reminded me that I had found a ghost for this wood during my researches; I was relieved to find that it was not the last man hanged for sheep-stealing stalking us, but a timid toad trundling back up to the wood from the reservoir below. Toad migration causes quite a hazard to toads and traffic using the busy A40. For some four or five mild damp evenings in late February, hundreds of toads, love-lorn but lethargic from long hibernation, amble and ramble 2 or 3 miles (3 to 5km) to the breeding grounds at Dowdeswell Reservoir. Thanks to the efforts of Dr Jeans and David Lewis and their ilk who patrol the A40 with flashlights and buckets helping the toads to cross the road in safety, life – both wild and human – is saved. A fast road surfaced by slow-moving toads is a great danger to drivers although the Department of Transport now post special 'Toad Migration' warning signs. The hard-surfaced road is very much favoured by the warty little amphibians so despised in folklore and offensive to other creatures that they have few predators, for here the males wait patiently for the females, oblivious of how today's traffic could wipe out the entire toad population of Dowdeswell in one season. The hefting instinct of the toad makes this a perennial problem, as those born in the reservoir will return to it when they, in turn, breed. Maybe, one day, this section of the Cotswold Way will be underpassed by toad tunnels as already constructed under major roads in Germany and Holland.

# 7
# Dowdeswell Reservoir to Charlton Kings Common

The Reservoir Inn makes a welcome stop along this section of the route which, unlike the north-wold Way, bypasses villages rather than goes through them. The Way heads off south just past the inn, opposite the reservoir, and is well signposted. Crossing the course of the old railway line, the edge of the pasture is followed to a gate at Lineover Wood. First bordering its eastern edge, the path then goes through it at a right angle. We found an odd clump of lilies of the valley on the ancient wood's floor. Fern and fungi were unfurling their fronds and frills and the soft green of certain spring was alive with birdsong. The wood clings tenaciously to the scarp, facing towards the Regency town of Cheltenham which vied with Bath as a fashionable spa, eventually earning the title of 'the merriest sick resort on earth'.

The Way continues up to Old Dole, then south-westward steeply to Ravensgate Hill and through a strip of firs on Wistley Hill. The view from here is superb.

There are plans afoot to reroute at a south-westerly angle to Charlton Kings Common, but legislation is a lengthy procedure so the official route at the time of going to press is to turn right on to the A436 for a mile's walk to Seven Springs. (See map). We took the unofficial path which has been favoured by many walkers, crossing the A436 through facing gates to Chatcombe Wood. Bluebells, massed blue against blue, and meadow saffron relieved the green between the trees; and holes of moles pitted the sandy banks. In the second field is a dewpond – a remnant of a vanished farming plan and the pond puddler's craft. My fancy was stirred by this now so rare feature which the old shepherds called a 'mist pond'. Needlehole to the left, north of Hilcot Wood, is another charming name for the 'wet hollow' from which it derived, although Upper Coberley just to the south of this marshy land was all but deserted in the Middle Ages through an insufficient water supply.

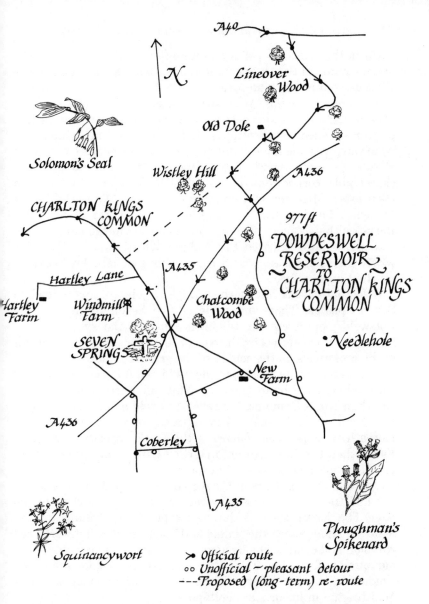

N

A40

Lineover Wood

Old Dole

Wistley Hill

A436

Solomon's Seal

CHARLTON KINGS COMMON

977ft
DOWDESWELL RESERVOIR
TO
CHARLTON KINGS COMMON

Hartley Lane

A435

Hartley Farm

Windmill Farm

Chatcombe Wood

•Needlehole

SEVEN SPRINGS

New Farm

A436

Coberley

A435

Squinancywort

Ploughman's Spikenard

> Official route
∘∘ Unofficial ~ pleasant detour
--- Proposed (long-term) re-route

Turning right onto the road it is another straightforward walk to Seven Springs, but having come round and about so far to avoid a stretch of road-walking along the A436, a little diversion to Coberley to visit the church of St Giles, approached through the arched doorway of a farmyard, enables you to see the likeness of Dick Whittington's mother. But the lady in wimple, hood and gown in the south chapel is a quite different character from the one we know in the classic pantomime, but the true story of the Gloucestershire boy who thrice became Lord Mayor of London is even more interesting. After serving a successful apprenticeship, Dick became the model merchant of the Middle Ages and court mercer of such great wealth that it is said the triumph of Agincourt was due in no small measure to his financial support of Henry V's costly wars. The legendary cat crops up in every conceivable cornerstone of his illustrious career, in stone in Gloucester Museum and mummified in the Natural History Museum, London. But at Coberley it is a horse of Sir Giles Berkeley that is remembered, for it is buried in the churchyard. His widow later married Sir William Whittington of Pauntley where their famous son was born, returning to Coberley Court for much of his childhood.

A footpath leads out of the village to join the main road to Seven Springs. There are at least five Seven Springs in the Cotswolds, but tradition will insist that in the sylvan hollow framed by fine beeches by the side of the A436, a few yards north of the crossroads, is the source of the great Thames.

The present route goes up to the A435 and A436 crossroads and then takes a left-hand track to Windmill Farm and thence to Charlton Kings Common. However, to avoid main-road walking, the Common can be reached by retracing to where the Coberley footpath met the road, following the track opposite to Hartley Farm, then turning right onto Hartley Lane to pick up the Way on the scrub-lined ascent to the Common.

Views to the right are of Cleeve Hill with the Malverns to the left and the hills of Wales beyond. The path keeps close to the edge. The distant scene is the townscape of Cheltenham and the Vale of Gloucester, the immediate one is of stitchwort, red campion and small scabious among the humps and hollows of the old quarry face. Ploughman's spikenard, so common on the Cotswolds, is quite different from the one which eulogised Dick Whittington in his original epitaph:

> 'Sweet as the spikenard's odours rise
> In fragrant columns to the skies,
> So sweet and fragrantly we see
> Ascend this Richard's memory.'

# 8
# Charlton Kings Common to Birdlip

Butterflies flutter by, spoilt for choice, and dogs lead their owners on for a bracing walk through gorse banks to the Common's summit. A trig point marks the summit of Charlton Kings Common. From here a path leads to the edge of the scarp to the Devil's Chimney, the most spectacular natural landmark on the route. Standing out from the freestone, the chimney is an oddity which excites academic speculation. The geologists say it is a quarryman's joke; the pinnacle of stone having been left as some sort of monument about 1780. In H. Ruff's *History of Cheltenham* he states: 'built by the Devil, as say the vulgar, it was no doubt built by shepherds in the frolic of an idle hour'. Then vulgar we may be; but we know a little more about shepherding folk who frolic not around the rocks chipping them about with their crooks! Serious erosion from the prevailing wet sou'westerlies has put the future of Old Nick's Chimney in doubt, a sum of £25,000 being needed for its immediate salvation. Saving the hill itself at the turn of the century brought the locals of Leckhampton out in force against an owner who had erected fences and employed a hunchback keeper to keep everyone off. But to the merry strains of a brass band, both fences and keeper were soon dealt with, and the fight for free access to the Hill was won. Until World War II, a bonfire was lit each year to commemorate the victory; now it is celebrated just by walkers walking freely.

The sheer faces and steep inclines are the result of extensive quarrying. Much of Regency Cheltenham was built from the freestone, quarried and worked 'freely' from Dead Man's Quarry below an Iron Age hillfort. It is difficult to imagine it teeming with stone-dusty quarrymen, firstly with creaking horse-drawn waggons, later with trams and railway engines. Over the last sixty years the dust has settled, the sounds of blasting and hammering have died away and a new generation of wildlife works and feeds and has its being among the tree and scrub grassland, healing the scars.

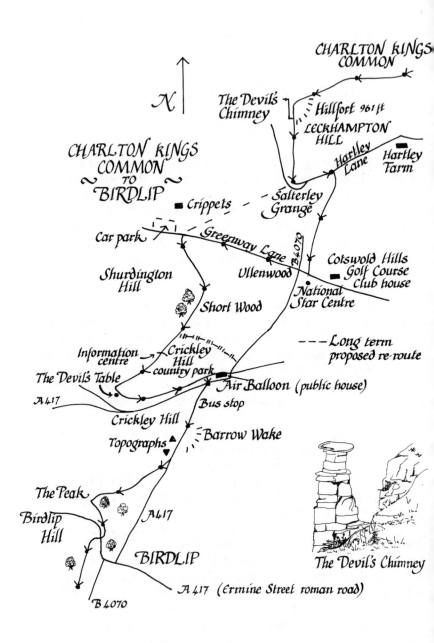

N

CHARLTON KINGS
COMMON

The Devil's
Chimney

Hillfort 961 ft
LECKHAMPTON
HILL

Hartley
Lane

Hartley
Farm

CHARLTON KINGS
COMMON
~ TO ~
BIRDLIP

Crippets

Salterley
Grange

Car park

Greenway Lane

B4070

Cotswold Hills
Golf Course
Club house

Shurdington
Hill

Ullenwood

Short Wood

National
Star Centre

--- Long term
proposed re-route

Information
centre

Crickley
Hill
country park

The Devil's Table

Air Balloon (public house)

A 417

Bus stop

Crickley Hill

Barrow Wake

Topographs

The Peak

Birdlip
Hill

A 417

BIRDLIP

A 417 (Ermine Street roman road)

B 4070

The Devil's Chimney

The path drops steeply to turn left onto the bottom of Hartley Lane where field hedgerows were bound together with giant convolvulus, and vetch veiled low-flowering brambles.* A smart green signpost points the way right to skirt the old sanatorium of Salterley Grange – now a block of flats. We picked huge bosses of elderflower from among those shading the narrow path, intoxicating the air with their heady scent. Three girls on horseback weaved their way along the track, the clip-clopping of hooves beating a country rhythm against the background of Cheltenham's traffic humming across the valley. Fine views of the Cotswold Hills golf course open out to the left as the route drops down to Ullenwood.

Turn right on the road. The National Star Centre, catering for disabled youth training, puts the Victorian mansion and its lovely grounds to splendid use. Past a stud farm, the B4070 is crossed to follow Greenway Lane, in the footsteps of the old sheep-drovers who walked these ways a thousand years ago when the abbey flocks of Gloucester roamed from Badgeworth to Coberley. There is a good view of the Devil's Chimney across to the right and a glimpse of Crippets, from whence Edward Wilson set off for his ill-fated expedition to the Antarctic with Captain Scott, just ahead and to the right of the ghostlike old army camp. A stile on the left leads across the headland of Shurdington Hill, with its ancient long barrow beyond the trees to the left but not on a public right of way. Keeping along the line of handsome beeches of Short Wood, the Crickley Hill Country Park is entered by a stile.

Crickley Hill encapsulates an exciting slice of prehistory. On this small site – a promontory of some 9 acres (3-6ha) – extensive excavation over 16 of the 21 years' project by some 2,500 volunteers has been one of the most successful archaeological undertakings in Britain. Successive sites on the hillfort commanding a strategic position on the westerly scarp line date from Early Neolithic farming settlements of 4000BC to 2000BC on the very tip, an occupation brought to a violent end by attacking archers. A fortified Iron Age village was then built about 600BC extending back onto the hill, and this was destroyed by fire. A century later a more complex fort defended a different-style

*A longterm proposal is to reroute the Way towards the car park in Greenway Lane – see map page 76 but follow way-marks.

village, but again suffered attack and destruction by fire. A stone circle or platform, believed to be of religious significance to the Neolithic community, has attracted considerable national interest. The artefacts are exhibited on site.

Together with Cooper's Hill and Coaley Peak, Crickley Hill is a regular patrol area for the volunteer Cotswold Wardens, to assist the Sites Warden in the interpretative and exhaustive task of reconciling the pressures on conservation and recreation. The Devil's Table, furnished from the eroded limestone, makes a fine natural table for a picnic.

The route leaves the hill close by the Air Balloon public house, crossing the A417 to go south along the pavement onto Barrow Wake to take in the expansive view sweeping the Vale of Gloucester. Topographs put the panorama and geology in perspective, and in Gloucester City Museum an exquisite bronze mirror found in the grave of an Iron Age lady reveals the arts of a lost and unrecorded people. The 'Birdlip Mirror', as it is known, is one of only two ever found of that period.

A recent diversion linking Barrow Wake to The Peak has improved the way, formerly affected by sand-slipping. Take time to enjoy the peace and view from The Peak. A motley bird population – finches, yellowhammers, blue-tits and great-tits, blackbirds and thrushes, finds a ready store of nuts and berries in the mixed woodland, with wild fruits for those of us who care to seek out the delights of gooseberry and raspberry in the shrubbery. Ermine Street, the old Roman road, cuts across the route, dividing The Peak from Birdlip. The village huddles on the steeply wooded hill, none of it old. The small church of St Mary was built as recently as 1957 in coursed rubble Cotswold stone, with a stained-glass window by my talented friend, Edward Payne. Such parochial pride may be incomprehensible to others, but the continuity of traditional craft skills breathes life into our heritage rather than relegating all to history and the 'years ago'.

Bringing the past alive is frequently practised hereabouts, in keeping with the closer alliance hill villages have with tradition than their valley cousins show. Birdlip schoolchildren weave their way with Pop Goes the Weasel and the Cuckoo Dance round the maypole and 'knock up the trees' to wake them up on May Day; and the Ermine Street legionaries march along the old Roman road to do their bit at village fêtes hailing from Witcombe – the 'wide valley' combe settled almost two thousand years ago.

# 9
# Birdlip to Prinknash

On Birdlip Hill the route enters the Witcombe Estate from a right-hand turn on the B4070. Here the walker is introduced to the beauty of the beechwoods which are the crowning glory of the Stroud Valley's stretch of the escarpment. Glorious in all seasons, late spring sunshine through the soft green of young beech leaves is magical; as it dances along the sandy woodland track the light glances on white helleborine, lily of the valley and angular Solomon's seal. The old Welsh drovers crossed this path, using a very ancient trackway onto Buckle Wood Common running parallel to Witcombe Wood, to avoid the 'Ketch Bar' tedium and toll at Birdlip turnpike.

About a mile further on, as the track forks at a bend, a spring on the right reminds one of how fresh water used to taste – strong, with a tang of iron. The springs on this rise were undoubtedly the reason for the Romans siting their villa a little downhill to the right, although they posed a threat to the foundations judging by the thickness of the walls. The water theme was translated in the mosaics – fish and dolphins in a seascape being quite different from the usual countryside scenes of Roman Gloucestershire. The waters of Witcombe Reservoirs winking from the valley below tease the time scale, but the homesick Latins may have glimpsed the shining swell of the Severn as it loops inland, and dreamt of warmer home waters. The villa is only rarely open to the public.

Beech banks against beech as far as the eye can see; to the left, beyond The Buckholt, are the woods of Cranham where, according to legend, a king lies buried on his golden throne, but as Nen's old Uncle Frank used to say: 'nobody didn't tell nobody nothing about nothing them-a-days' – the translation of which hides the pretty wit of the countryman and, who knows, even more! Keeping to the route of the waymarked path does not keep the mind on course and I couldn't help rolling the name Cranham over and over, as a child will a sweet, when Nen, fascinated with placenames, asked what it meant. Like her old Uncle Frank, she speaks Gloucestershire 'as she should be spoke' but can also

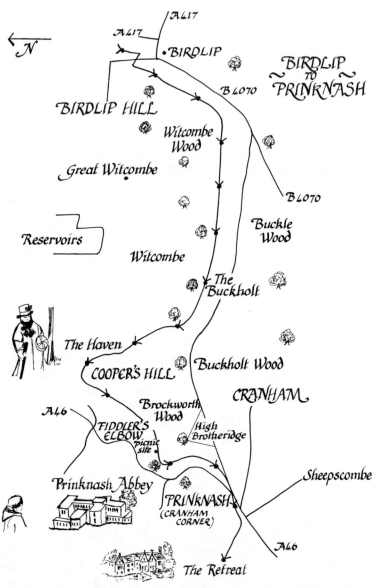

N

A417

A417

•BIRDLIP

*BIRDLIP
TO
PRINKNASH*

B4070

BIRDLIP HILL

Witcombe
Wood

Great Witcombe

B4070

Reservoirs

Witcombe

Buckle
Wood

The
Buckholt

The Haven

COOPER'S HILL

Buckholt Wood

CRANHAM

A46

Brockworth
Wood

FIDDLER'S
ELBOW

picnic
site

High
Brotheridge

Prinknash Abbey

PRINKNASH
(CRANHAM
CORNER)

Sheepscombe

A46

The Retreat

outmalaprop Mrs Malaprop, so Cranham became *Camlann*. Fired
by the royal genealogists' researches to forge a hereditary line
from King Arthur to young Prince William – who lives 'just over
Jack's mother's' (as we say 'a little distance yonder') – the
Arthurian legend became tantalisingly local. Records speak of
Arthur's last battle at Camlann after he crossed the Severn.

As we left the wood, our immediate attention was caught by a lovely Cotswold cottage, the views opening out, and the delights of The Haven tea garden where you sign the visitor's book. And we wondered again at our fellow Cotsallers who hurtle down Cooper's Hill chasing a 7lb (3.2kg) cheese down its one-in-one gradient. The prize is a cheese – Double Gloucester, of course. The tradition of cheese-rolling is thought to be rooted in a pagan midsummer ceremony whereby a wheel or round object, representing the sun, was rolled down a hill and, when caught, symbolised the arrest of the shortening days: the festival is now held at spring bank holiday. Another theory is that it is in celebration of a victory – and as the records indicate the custom to date back at least 1,300 years, why not Camlann? The feeling of antiquity is strengthened by the site of what is thought to be an Iron Age settlement farther along on High Brotheridge. A Victorian programme lifts the sepia off the old photos to show staid gents and stayed matrons at such junketings as:

2 cheeses to be ron for (down the hill)
1 plain cake to be green for (the best, or funniest, grin through
  a horse collar being the winner)
1 plain cake to be jumpt in the bag for (a kind of sack race)
Horings to be dipt in the toob for (oranges floated in a tub of salt
  water had to be caught in the mouth)
Set of ribbons to be danced for
Shimey to be ron for (girls run for a chemise)
Belt to be rosled for
A bladder of snuff to be chatred for by hold wimming (it is not
  clear whether the winner was the old woman who chattered
  the longest or the loudest)

The ribbons danced for by the lasses, and the belt wrestled for by the lads, were those worn by the Master of Ceremonies. He is still a colourful figure in his white smock and black top hat decked with red, white and blue ribbons, with matching flower buttonhole. The grinning and wrestling and chattering are replaced by tugs-of-war, and sweet-scrambles from the maypole. The pole is traditionally one from Witcombe Wood, thus protecting the Commoners' rights. Those who have rights tied to their properties still enjoy the ancient privileges.

A rather superfluous notice prohibits driving on the hill – a feat nearing impossibility one would think, although Reverend Witts, in *The Diary of a Cotswold Parson*, writes of travelling on the outside of the Stroud coach down Cooper's Hill in a heavy storm of mingled snow, sleet and rain.

Nature trails are laid out from Cooper's Hill through Brock-worth Wood and around High Brotheridge, with a picnic area where Fiddler's Elbow leans into the scarp edge. Herb robert rose in great banks in clearings with woodruff and sanicle alongside the tracks. A flash of fallow deer started off as we penetrated deep into the wood to pick at the sweet wild strawberries. Beech still dominates the woodland scene right into Buckholt.

Beautiful as Buckholt is, it is Prinknash (pronounced Prinage) which attracts immediate attention, for through a clearing on the edge of the wood the starkly simple shape of the abbey stands sentinel to the faith and tenacity of monastic life in a modern world. Clad in the richly coloured oolitic limestone quarried at Guiting in the heart of the Cotswolds, it literally glows like a golden jewel in the lush green parkland below. It is worth the short diversion from the waymarked route to turn right at Cranham Corner to visit Prinknash Abbey which stands off the A46. Apart from being the only monastery in the Cotswolds, it is our only working abbey.

It was high summer when we met up with our producer for the next programme. Bees bumbled along the blowsy blossoms, intoxicated by the sweet scents of sun-baked herbs in the Regency walled monastery garden overlooking the Severn Vale. The grey-gabled grange which has served the abbots of Gloucester, the royal Tudors, generations of Gloucestershire gentry and the

*Walking through Buckholt Wood*

*The Grange from the monastery garden, Prinknash*

Benedictine monks, each in their season from the Middle Ages, stands like a venerable patriarch, on a rise cloaked by vibrant beech, ½ mile (.8km) distant, but not divorced, from the new abbey gilded and gracious across the valley. My mind was still full of my recent conversation with Father Abbot Aldhelm in the peace of the parlour, which had continued as we walked through the tranquil twilight to vespers in the crypt. The chiming call of the abbey bells brought the brothers hardly hurrying, but purpose bent, from kitchen and cloister, pottery and forge, farm and garden, study cell and incense-still to their devotions. For over forty years the lone figure of a white-robed monk has rung the heavy bells suspended in their iron frame on the lawn in front of the abbey: the bells await their belfry; the monks await their church. The crypt, consecrated as their temporary church, is almost entirely furnished by the monks themselves; the clean cut lines and acute angles of altar and balustrade, choir stalls and crucifix are softened only by the warm buff of the stone, the same stone which shaped Stanway Manor. It says something for the versatility of the stone, and the skill of master masons, that such extremes of the ornate and the austere can be produced with equal excellence. The early evening sun patterned the white robes with kaleidoscopic colour transmitted through the modern stained-glass windows, shifting shape as the monks moved through their low Latin chants. It made an indelible impression on me; the movement in the crypt seemed analogous to the community's move to the Cotswolds.

Thomas Dyer Edwardes on his conversion to Catholicism in 1924, invited the Benedictines of Caldey to make a foundation at his estate at Prinknash Park. As the monks left the island to

*Bellringing outside the new abbey,*
*Prinknash*

make the rough crossing across Caldey Sound their boat passed under a rainbow. They did not find the fabled gold at the end of the rainbow, but the seam of clay at the foot of the Cotswold hills, revealed when they were digging the foundations for the new abbey, has brought them both fortune and fame, for the distinctive Prinknash pottery is the principal source of the monastery's income. Prinknash has no parish, wealthy endowments or school to support it. A great percentage of production is now for export – a far cry from the early days when Brothers Thomas and Basil first threw the thick Cotswold clay on a wheel in a garden shed as a tentative step towards producing a couple of pots to add a few pence to the abbey's housekeeping.

When we were there, Father Basil had just completed work on sculpting a statue of the Virgin and Child for the Roman Catholic Church at Painswick commemorating its Golden Jubilee. Three of his father's paintings hang in the calefactory. My childhood cartoonist hero, Heath Robinson, had captured the monks repairing the old manor house which they had outgrown, and building the new abbey, as only he could; the pictures of cranks and pulleys hauling up hammer-wielding monks, aided by precariously perched brothers on laced up ladders did not seem incongruous somehow for a monastery is a microcosm of a community with all its human frailities and strengths. And Prinknash is rather special. It has to be to survive a thousand years of monasticism and integrate into twentieth-century society.

# 10
# Prinknash to Painswick

From Prinknash Corner the route crosses the A46 and turns right just before the Royal William (so named long before *the* royal William came to the already royalty-favoured Cotswolds). Ascending into Pope's Wood, the track comes out alongside the fairway of the golf course. We had mistaken a waymark for the white lichen which spots the stone boulders and posts, but a friendly golfer, obviously used to straying Cotswold Wayfaring folk, redirected us. The most north-westerly margin has to be taken, however, to get to Painswick Beacon where the Iron Age people built yet another hillfort, fortified in Saxon times, and a bleak even if relatively safe campsite for royalist troops during the Civil War siege of Gloucester. It is a place for electric storms: the effect of forked lightning splitting pink-edged navy-blue storm clouds massed over the Severn Vale beyond is startling. Proposals for re-routing to cross the Beacon are in hand.

The Way winds a joyous course along a wooded shelf and Nen told us tales of how all hell was let loose in Paradise when some misguided body tried to change the name of the tiny hamlet below the tree line. Tradition has it that when Charles I took refuge in

*Severn Vale from Painswick Beacon*

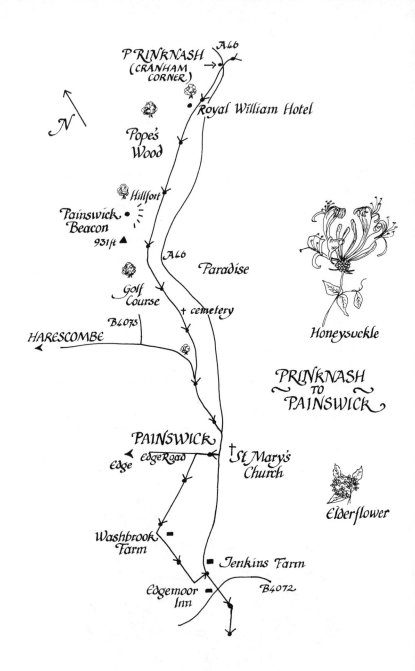

P RINKNASH
(CRANHAM
CORNER)

A46

Royal William Hotel

Pope's
Wood

Hillfort

Painswick
Beacon
931ft ▲

A46

Paradise

Golf
Course

B4073

HARESCOMBE

+ cemetery

PRINKNASH
~ TO ~
PAINSWICK

PAINSWICK

Edge   EdgeRoad

† St Mary's
Church

Washbrook
Farm

Jenkins Farm

Edgemoor
Inn

B4072

N

Honeysuckle

Elderflower

the sheltered combe he exclaimed, 'This is Paradise'; so woe betide those who say it is not. The inn was appropriately called the Adam and Eve. At one time it belonged to Godsells Brewery which prompted the local ditty:

> Adam and Eve in (n) Paradise –
> God sells beer!

Sited on the curve of the busy main road, with no car park, the Adam and Eve lost its custom and closed. So there is now no beer in Paradise. But my champagne, made from elderflowers picked earlier along the Way, back-bone pie (an old Campden speciality), and newly-dug potatoes cooked with pitch-eyed beans, followed by wild strawberries made feast enough for us that summer's day we strolled down to Paradise.

The route continues along the ridgeline above, through alpine-like scenery before opening out above the golf clubhouse on a bank where wild thyme grows. A leafy lane leads down to the main road to enter Painswick.

*Walking the Painswick Valley*

Painswick valleys are sheer poetry and Painswick itself is their crowning glory – a small town of pearl-grey stone characteristically and structurally Cotswold, its strong angular lines built in light sensitive limestone. There is a grace about Painswick that has earned it the title of 'Queen of the Cotswolds', and it is a happy coincidence that it is set at the halfway stage of the Cotswold Way – geographically, architecturally and historically.

As the Way turns left past Gyde's Orphanage, now affiliated to the National Children's Home, it follows along Gloucester Street,

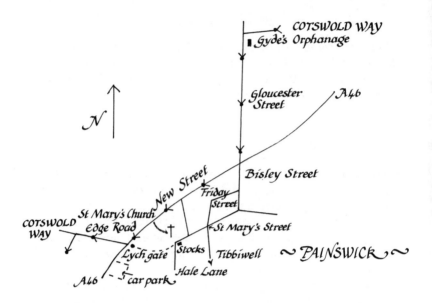

the main thoroughfare when 'Wicke' was but a Saxon village on the saltway. Pain Fitzjohn, who owned the village in the twelfth century, personalised it. Subsequent Lords of the Manor made their mark on history mainly by the violence of their demise; battles, suicide, accidents and murders plucked them off. No wonder one, when told of his release from the Tower, died of relief! Shakespeare immortalised the deaths of the Earl of Shrewsbury and his son at the hands of the French in *Henry IV*; Lord Lisle, a grandson, met his fate nearer home – at Nibley Green farther along the route; and the hated Sir Anthony Kingston got his deserts by questionable means while crossing the Thames at Lechlade on his way to Coberley Court for trial.

Painswick, as we know it today, is the legacy of the Cotswold wool trade when the economy shifted from farming raw fleece to manufacturing cloth. The medieval merchants of the Staple disappeared; their place taken by Elizabethan Merchant Adventurers. The great monastic flocks were dispersed to be absorbed into the new mixed-farming patterns, and the vast sheepwalks of the north wolds were turned by the plough to more profitable arable yields. Spinners, not shepherds, were the new link between fleece and fortune; but it was still a merchant's world, and the substantial stately houses which are the beauty of the town are those of the mercers and clothiers who grew rich on the sweated labour of those who worked in the dark mills

secluded in the deep valley bottoms below. The natural advantages of the valley springs, the presence of fuller's earth, and the
ready supply of Cotswold fleece were knit together by exiled
Huguenots who, seeking refuge in the West Country, taught the
weavers the intricacies of 'huswyff's, narrow and brode wayver'.
It was the latter, broadweaving, which eventually made the
Stroud valleys the home of the famous West of England cloth-
making in which, during the boom years, half the population was
involved, including the children.

Two deciding factors which brought the Civil War raging
around these quiet ways were, firstly, the strategic position of the
Cotswolds in the king's passage from his headquarters at Oxford
to his safe South Wales seat and, secondly, the economic
importance of the area's cloth trade held, then, in the hands of
strongly parliamentarian merchants. That Charles I stayed in
the town is evidenced by a proclamation which he issued from
'our court at Payneswicke'; that there was a skirmish, when a
group of Royalists flushed out some two hundred Roundheads
with blazing torches and cannonballs, can be seen on the tower
and walls of the parish church.

The severity and distress of the depression in the cloth trade
are buried with those who suffered the storm and aftermath of the
Industrial Revolution. Slow and loathe to change, the Cotswold
mill owners and workers did not, or could not, come to terms with
the new machinery which would speed up the processes and cut
the misery of their arduous work; so, unlike their canny north-
country competitors they lost their hold on the trade and a whole
way of life. A Painswick clothier, Daniel Packer, wrote to his
London factor in 1768 that his cloth was 'honestly worth £11 and
cannot be afforded under . . . we shall have fewer Clothiers
another year, . . . last Tuesday Sam Haines shot himself through
the Head; he was deeply in debt for Wooll'.

To pad out the diminishing profits, the owners reduced the
wages of the workers, as a particularly erudite appeal from one
George Risby in a report of 1839 reveals:

Our hours of work are thirteen per day for 12s 6d a week . . .
the reason why my children do not earn more is because our
abb is spun on bobbins . . . we are ten in family and we are very
destitute of clothes . . . The word of God tells me I shall get
bread by the sweat of my brow, but I have the sweat of the brow
and not the bread, and all through oppression.

The distressed state of the weavers even distressed the police who were sent to the wretched homes to search for stolen yarn or slinge. One statement said: 'not one family out of ten can attend church in consequence of their ragged condition', what meals they could afford being 'potatoes with a bit of flick or suet'.

Despite the radical changes in the clothmaking industry it took over two centuries to completely run down. The trade was as tenacious to its traditions as its hard-worked hardy workers were to life, the Painswick creed being 'Too poor to live but too healthy to die'. Many severed their ties with their Cotswold roots and emigrated, others moved to the mining areas or found work on the newly developing railways. Even so, a Board of Education report of 1910 stated: 'the wool industry carried on almost entirely in the Stroud area is still considerable, clothmaking and dyeing providing much employment'.

Mills that no longer produced cloth became factories making such things as walking sticks and pins, and the whole central area of the Cotswold Way from Painswick to Wotton-under-Edge became industrialised. The Board's survey showed some 60,000 persons engaged in industry compared with 25,000 in agriculture, and to meet the demands technical education and evening classes were introduced. Of the 25 mills that once hummed through the peak period of the wool industry on the waters in the valleys between Painswick and Stroud, only 2 today still produce the fine West of England woollen cloth on which the fame and fortunes of the area depended for almost 400 years; both within the environs of Stroud.

As the route progresses through the pretty town of Painswick, its past is neatly wrapped up in the stone of its buildings and whispers across the centuries in a name. The straightforward through-route bears right down New Street – well, at least it was new in 1430 – past the timber-framed Post Office dating from about 1500 and a medley of architecturally interesting buildings with The Beacon attributed to John Wood the younger, whose work will be met with again at the end of the Walk in Bath; and St Mary's slender spire beckoning you on to sample its beauties. But it would be a pity not to allow a little time to walk round the town rather than just through it.

Over the crossroads into Bisley Street, where packhorse entrances, now blocked in, can be spotted at The Chur – a former coffee tavern, and Wickstone – whose cellars are reputedly haunted by the restless ghost of a clothier searching for his lost fortune. The buildings date back to the fourteenth century, contemporary with Little Fleece, which is all that remains of a former inn on what is still the original main road through the town. Across the road is Friday Street, taking its name from the market day. Houses on the right embody the steep gables, mullioned windows and dripmoulds that are so characteristically Cotswold. Built in the native stone, they contrast so pointedly with those on the opposite side, built hurriedly in more inferior style and materials following an air raid on the town in 1941.

*Tibbiwell Street ~ Painswick*

On the left from the Cross, Tibbiwell Street descends steeply between more picturesque houses 300 years old, to Painswick Stream lined with the old cloth mills. The clacking and creaking of the heavy looms have died away, and today they are private houses with a public past; only Pin Mill survives. This is Laurie Lee country. In the next valley, but in the same parish, is where he sipped cider with Rosie; nearly every comely wench in the Slad valley claiming to have been the celebrated Rosie. The whole area is a walker's paradise, and due acknowledgement was accorded to the Cotswold Wardens for their help in enabling Painswick to win the Footpaths Heritage competition.

Returning to the town through the churchyard, take note of the 'spectacle' stocks just right of the entrance. These leg irons, made about 1840, are thought to be unique in the British Isles. They were certainly used as a deterrent within living memory when 'young Mary', who had peculiar powers of healing animals on the strength of being born a 'chime child' (at the stroke of midnight on a Good Friday), was whispered about in suspicious tones by local folk. The squire, whose dog Mary cured so miraculously, intervened and threatened to have the slanderers put in the stocks.

In the Cotswold comprehension, all phenomena not readily understood to be the works of nature are ascribed to those of the Deity or the Devil and here, as any Painswickian will tell you, the old Devil kills off the hundredth yew. The yews, most of which are 200 years old, are both feature and folklore of the churchyard. 'Long-yudded scholards' (learned folk) try to point out that because some have divided and some grown together it is difficult to count them accurately, but the old wags always win on that point because no two people agree on the same total.

Apart from the avenues of the legendary ninety-nine yews, the churchyard is furnished with an unequalled collection of monumentally interesting tombs – tea-caddie, chest, pyramidical, octagonal, sarcophagus, and the table-tops so beloved by the old poachers and smugglers as a safe store. Ornate and elaborate, the like will never be made again. A 'tomb trail' pamphlet is available from the church.

The church itself is elegant and spacious, with numerous fine features both old and new from far and near. The crucifix was made in Oberammergau, world-famous for its passion play; the south-aisle iron screen was made in Nuremburg; the sanctuary lamps are by the Harts of Chipping Campden whom we met at the start of our walk; and the west window by Edward Payne from just across the valley at Box. The symbolic ship at the end of the west aisle is actually a model of Sir Francis Drake's *Bonaventure* which fought the Spanish Armada. We shall meet with one of Drake's sailors farther along the route.

It was a storm-swept September Sunday when we set off from Painswick for the next leg of our walk after joining in the annual Clipping Ceremony, which has nothing to do with trimming the yews as so often purported. Heralded by a slightly breathless band from Avening village, the clergy and scarlet-robed choir progressed round the churchyard as generations have throughout the ages; and we joined hands for the Saxon *ycleping* (embracing) of the church to the special 'Clipping' hymn. Nearly everyone

sported some floral decoration. Little boys in best suits wore
discrete buttonholes like their Dads'; pretty girls sported mob-
caps sprigged with blossoms, some wore garlands of late summer
garden rosebuds and early autumn hedgerow rosehips; a bemused
old boxer dog had a collar of chrysanthemums; and the vicar of
Randwick, who got the blame for the inclement weather, received
a flower-decked basketful of buns for giving such a good address.
He was knowledgeable about such ceremonies, with his own
parish proud of their Runnick Wap and cheese-rolling tradition.
We joined the queue inside the church for a Painswick bun – a
large spicy bun made specially for the festival service by the local
baker, and the children each received two bob as a tenpence piece.
Nen recorded her childhood memories for the radio programme,
but did not divulge that she and the cousins from Stroud paid
their devotions annually at Painswick for the bun and, in those
days, a tanner!

*Painswick church and lychgate*

As we left the church by way of the pretty lych gate, built of old
timbers from the belfry which was damaged when the spire fell
down a century ago, the deep-seated rivalry between 'strutting
Stroud and Painswick proud' again reared its hoary head.
Someone remarked on the glorious peal of twelve bells – only

about thirty other churches boasting that number. 'Ah,' said another, 'but 'twere only ten til Stroud got ther'n from six to ten, so Painswick had to best us by going whole hog. The bells be like their bomb. They a-babbled about how 'ee dropped one yur so they must've been more important than we but as Jarge sed, it might 'ave dropped at Painswick but ol' Jerry must've put his thumb on the button at Stroud.' We recognised the couple from paying their homage and collecting their bun – Cotswold folk don't change much!

# 11
# Painswick to Middle Yard

The Way leaves Painswick opposite the lych gate, follows Edge Road and then turns left over a stile. The field walking, in pleasant open countryside, passes Washbrook Farm which originated as a cloth mill on Spoonbed Brook. Keeping to the hedgeline and crossing a footbridge, the route ascends to skirt Jenkins Farm, then takes a right turn onto the road and crosses the B4072 by the Edgemoor Inn. Right at the wall corner, then left, takes you along the southerly edge of the birch trees. The ascent up Rudge Hill common allows a fine view back to Painswick against its wooded backcloth. Keeping right at Scottsquar on Edge Common the composition of the distinctive Lower Inferior Oolite is seen to advantage in the *sceot* (steep) *quar* (the Cotswold term for quarry). Cross the minor road which leads to Edge, and take a left-angled track to the north-facing edge of Halliday Wood on route to Haresfield Beacon.

For some 2 miles (3.2km) the Way follows the sweeping curve of the wood. The prickly cases of the horse chestnuts were just splitting open to spill mahogany-coloured conkers in our path. A hexagonal house set deep in the wood on the right is both quaint and curious for this environment. Turn right onto the byroad to the northern tip of the wood. A stone-built well-head beside Cliffwell House speaks of its original purpose:

> Whoer the Bucketful upwindeth, let him bless God,
>> who water findest.
> Yet water here but small availeth,
>> Go seek that well which never failest.

Here, the Way goes left to continue the woodland walk. Cromwell's Stone on the scarp edge overlooks the Vale of Gloucester. Plain and angular, its commemoration is more curious than its composition, considering it was the king's army who raised the siege on Gloucester on 5 September 1643 – the date on the stone.

Beatrix Potter might well have been inspired by this wooded

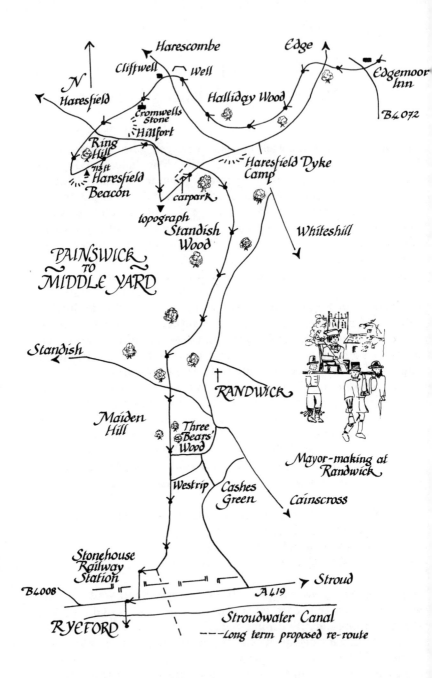

N

Harescombe

Cliffwell    Well    Edge

Haresfield    Halliday Wood    Edgemoor Inn

B4072

Cromwells Stone
Hillfort

Ring Hill

713 ft
Haresfield Beacon    carpark    Haresfield Dyke Camp

topograph    Whiteshill

Standish Wood

PAINSWICK
TO
MIDDLE YARD

Standish

RANDWICK

Maiden Hill

Mayor-making at Randwick

Three Bears' Wood

Westrip    Cashes Green    Cainscross

Stonehouse Railway Station    Stroud

B4008    A419

RYEFORD    Stroudwater Canal
---- Long term proposed re-route

hill area studded with storybook names during her stay at the romantic old Harescombe Grange, about 4 furlongs (.8km) in the deep valley of Daniell's Brook. Her journey to Gloucestershire opposed by her possessive parents, as she reveals in her journal: 'It was so much an event in the eyes of my relatives that they made it appear an undertaking to me, and I began to think I would rather not go.' Had she not come to the Cotswold cousins in 1894 and wrote about 'a very pretty story I heard in the country', the story world would have been the poorer and Mr Prichard, who died in 1934, would never have passed into our folklore as the Tailor of Gloucester. As Beatrix herself wrote of the story: 'And the queerest thing about it . . . it is true! At least about the tailor, the waistcoat and the No more twist.' The illustrations are based on sketches she made in the area; one of the tailor was of the coachman's son at Harescombe, and snippets from inside Cotswold cottages included an old settle, a four-poster bed and a dresser.

Haresfield Beacon promontory encloses a hillfort and an ancient encampment at Ring Hill. Historians will know that the Romans left a pot of some three thousand bronze coins and scanty evidence of their occupation of this strategic point on the spur; geologists will seize footholds in the stony north-west scarp face to examine the strata where Upper Lias sands meet the Inferior Oolite. The view from the Beacon is magnificent: the Severn, glinting as it winds its serpentine course through the Vale of Gloucester, draws the eye on to the Forest of Dean.

The southern scarp edge descends steeply, touched briefly by the Haresfield road, and then the route is through trees and a path on the left. A stone in memory 'of all foxes' reminds walkers that this is Berkeley Hunt country. Veering right to the southerly spot marked by a topograph, then left to the National Trust car park, an ancient track in Standish Wood is followed down to a stile. The Way loops to the right along the ridge path. We were lucky enough to walk this way at Michaelmas, when lingering summer and advancing autumn joined forces to show off late blooms and early berries. Honeysuckle and black bryony tangled with the thinner undercover, and holly made dark shiny patches between the pungent smelling yew; but it was still the beech that flaunted its fiery beauty for well over a mile.

The extensive wood ends as a kind of punctuation point to the pastoral prettiness of the Painswick valleys. Crossing over the track to a gate, the Way goes over Maiden Hill, through another gate, then left to a stone stile into the storybook-sized Three Bears' Wood. Across the minor road the route descends the bank by means of stiles to the houses at Westrip in the suburbs of the Stroud Valley.*

Turning right, the Way follows a short stretch of road, then angles off left at a stone stile to descend pasture-land keeping the hedgeline as a guide. The industrial and urban environs can be a shock to senses so long attuned to the calm of the countryside. Derelict cars around an old brickworks are best hurried past. A footbridge traverses the Stonehouse railway line; past a sports field a prettily hedged path leads under the school footbridge, then left off the A419 main road to cross the Stroudwater Canal. Ivy was in full yellow-green flower against the old stone bridge, and the plants on the bank sides were already assuming individuality from the mass of fading summer green, with rusts and golds and purplish reds picking out leaf shapes and enhancing stem lines.

Stroud is 1½ miles (2.4km) away. A town of narrow streets on very steep hills, its industrial past overspilt into the valley bottom leaving muddle and uncertainty in its wake, in which the passing of its former importance was erased and painfully new and utilitarian units erected hastily in its place. The railways that brought the coal too late to convert the water-driven mills to steam as used by the more astute Yorkshire mill owners, also brought dull slate and brick and concrete for the new buildings. Cheaper and quicker to build than the hard-hewn native stone; time has not made the incongruity less conspicuous.

To make a navigable link from the tidal Severn to the Thames and on to London, therefore a crossing of southern England by water from west to east, was the aspiration of the eighteenth-century industrialists. The Stroudwater Company spearheaded the scheme and its 8 mile (13km) long canal, with 13 locks, was fully opened in 1779, putting Stroud in an enviable position ahead of all other Cotswold wool towns. To Wallbridge in Stroud came the fleece fresh from the farms; from the mills of Stroud to the Severn at Framilode went the bales of broadcloth. Stroud scarlets and Uley blues became famous throughout Europe, and

*Another longterm proposal is to reroute the Way on the easterly side to cross Selsey Common – see map page 102 but follow waymarks.

the wealth from the 150 mills along the River Frome and its tributaries made this the 'Golden Valley' of the Cotswolds. The last working barge used the canal here in 1941, a century after the majority of the mills had been closed because of the cloth trade depression.

Soon the Way passes over another bridge at Ryeford, the rye harvest of yore having been carted over a ford hereabouts before the Frome's waters were harnessed to the corn – and then the cloth-mill wheels. Here, as a great memorial to the Stroud Valley's golden industrial age is Stanley Mill; not just a monument, it is a full working mill – one of the only two producing woollen cloth in the area. Records show a mill on this site before Domesday, probably for corn. The first textile mill to full (mill) the woollen cloth hand-woven by the local cottage weavers was established about 1550 by the Clutterbuck family. A gig mill, using locally grown teasels for raising the nap, was added a century later.

The huge cone-headed fuller's teasel is now difficult to find as a wild flower. I grow a handful for myself and the bumble bees; hive bees seem to get into a soporofic stupor from the mauve and white flowers. Teasel-growing was an ancillary business of the cloth trade in Gloucestershire. Up to 3,000 teasel heads would be used on a 40yd (36m) roll of dense-textured West Country broadcloth, and as teasels throve better on 'teart' soil unsuitable for pastureland, such a prickly crop made sound agrarian sense as well as servicing the country's major industry. The last crop was recorded in the early 1950s. The finest broadcloth finish could mean teaselling and shearing some twenty-five times. It was a Stroud clothmaker, John Lewis, who in 1815 invented a rotary nap-trimmer to replace the hand-shearing of the raised nap – and thus spearheaded the design for the rotary lawn-mower.

The present Stanley Mills were built in 1813. Marling & Evans who now own them think it was probably the world's first fireproof textile factory, certainly England's first. Brick replaced traditional stone walls, but it is the stone floors suspended on a cast-iron framework which attracts home and overseas students interested in the Industrial Revolution. Locally, and certainly for me, the most exciting inheritance of such a long-established mill is that all the processes – carding, spinning, dyeing, blending, weaving and finishing of virgin wools – are still carried on in the heart of Cotswold wool country. Some sixty workers now produce well over 6,000yd (5,486m) a week of fine West of England woollen cloth. Today it carries the seal of the Woolmark standard; where for centuries each piece was certified by the distinctive mark of the Clutterbuck clothier family.

Elegant and gabled Stanley House, just past the mill on the right, illustrates the wealth and standing of the Clutterbucks for whom it was built four hundred years ago. A small stone-built roundhouse stored the wool shuttles. St George's Church, with many Norman features and a nave wagon-roof, close by, is worth a short detour. There are monuments to the Clutterbucks and other leading families of King's Stanley, and in the churchyard a barmaid's sad end is recorded on a copper plaque on one of the flat gravestones:

> Twas as she tript from cask to cask,
> In at a bung hole quickly fell,
> Suffocation was her task,
> She had not time to say farewell.

They do not write history like that on tombstones any more!

The Way skirts the old village of King's Stanley – the prefix distinguishing this *stan leah* (stony clearing) crown property from Leonard Stanley, a little to the west, which belonged to the ancient priory of St Leonard's – by turning left just beyond Stanley Mill over a stile to a track leading through Peckstreet Farm. Stiles and waymarks lead you across the fields; go left at the old chapel then right to the hardly-a-village of Middle Yard.

# 12
# Middle Yard to Cam Long Down

Pairs and terraces of stone-built weavers' cottages give character to the straggling hamlet which takes its name from the sixteenth-century Middle Farmhouse. The shop just to the right is well-frequented by walkers. The route goes right through to touch Coombe Lane, then a narrow lane leads to a stile, and a field with a steep ascent, to join Pen Lane at its southerly point and enjoy yet more beechwood walking. Wending westward, the woodlands of Pen Hill continue into Stanley Wood which runs for 1½ miles (2.4km) along the scarp slope.

Stanley Wood was bought recently by the Woodland Trust. Established just over a decade ago as a registered charity, the Trust has grown into a major conservation organisation with a membership of some 41,000 – a measure of the interest and concern generated in recent years to not only conserve woods of special interest but also to make them available for recreation. Major replanting between 1950 and 1974 introduced a wide range of species, half the wood being conifers. A programme is underway to re-establish a predominantly broadleaved woodland again, and this is being partly achieved already by natural forces. For where the odd larch and pine have failed, there has been a regeneration of ash and the dominant beech, both supporting a high density of the invertebrate life which provides a vital food supply for the robins, blackbirds and songthrushes that add delight to dawn and dusk walking.

Gliders soar over from Nympsfield – a tract of open country where the land ends on the southern side of the wood. Nympsfield folk used to celebrate St Margaret's Day, 20 July, with 'Hegpeg Dump' – the Cotswold name for plum pudding.

The Way reaches the tapering tail of woodland at Buckholt Wood by an old quarry with wayfaring trees along the top, and enters Coaley Peak picnic site by the information centre. Here, information on the immediate area is well illustrated and we learn that Buckholt, meaning beechwood, derives from the German *buch* (book), originally of beechwood boards rather like

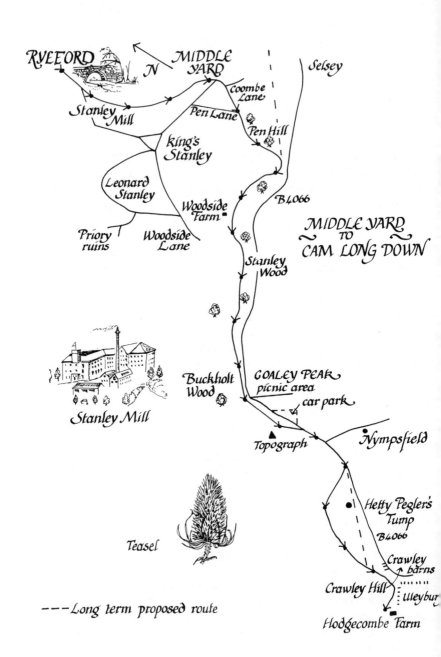

RYEFORD

N

MIDDLE YARD

Selsey

Stanley Mill

Coombe Lane

Pen Lane

Pen Hill

king's Stanley

B4066

Leonard Stanley

Woodside Farm

MIDDLE YARD
TO
CAM LONG DOWN

Priory ruins

Woodside Lane

Stanley Wood

Stanley Mill

Buckholt Wood

COALEY PEAK
picnic area

car park

Topograph

Nympsfield

Hetty Pegler's Tump
B4066

Teasel

Crawley barns

Crawley Hill

Weybur

Hodgecombe Farm

– – – Long term proposed route

our early chap-boards. Reading the woodland character and plant life is aided by nature trails managed by the Gloucestershire Trust for Nature Conservation; the quarry land belongs to the National Trust. A plan of the Nympsfield long barrow is more elucidatory than a close up examination, but it is nearby just south-west of the picnic site. It is an interesting example of the early true-entrance Severn-Cotswold type, as compared with the false-entrance style of Belas Knap, but is not so well preserved. Most of the dry-stone walling is present-day renovator's rather than the Neolithic builder's. The Celts named it 'shrine-field' so the barrow must still have been an impressive sight in its day. Then it deteriorated and was shunned by local folk who nursed the tradition that it was a leper's cell. It was excavated in 1937, and the sight of some thirteen skeletons all sitting down must have been somewhat spooky. The view of Berkeley Vale from the scarp edge is expansive and explained on a topograph.

Leaving the picnic site by way of a kissing gate, the old quarry path leads on a little way up Frocester Hill. Scrub bushes along the quarry were hung about with Traveller's-Joy, or Old Man's Beard, soft like discarded gossamer shawls.

Bear right onto the B4066, then right again to enter the woodland and descend along the old track to the foot of the scarp where it touches Tickshill road. Veer left to regain the woodland – dense with oak, ash, hazel and sycamore, whose huge leaves splash the mossed and ferned floor with fairy plates of autumn gold – and the last of the fine long barrows is on the high ground left of the track.*

Hetty Pegler's Tump takes its name from the seventeenth-century owners of the field in which the chambered long barrow is sited. We were lucky enough to arrive there at the same time as another couple who, well primed and therefore armed with the key and a torch, aided our crawl in – the entrance is about 3ft (1m) high, but the passage inside is slightly higher. Such difficulty in entering did not deter the Romans who were not only nosy but careless too, for they left fragments of pottery as evidence. And was it a Lancastrian or a Yorkist who sought refuge in this dank and eerie cairn and dropped his silver groat? We were all relieved to emerge into the crisp autumnal air, but

*In the longterm, rerouting is planned to take the Way directly alongside Hetty Pegler's Tump – see map.

agreed the monument was impressive as a link with our ancestors who had returned to the Mother Earth's womb when they had seen the sun set over the Severn for the last time. We made our farewells and godspeed for our respective journeys, they northwards and we southwards; we thanked them for bringing the key and they thanked us for returning it – each saving the other a backtrack of some ½ mile (.8km) to the cottage at Crawley Barns at the top of the hill.

For those with a predilection for promontory forts, Uleybury offers one of the best examples in the British Isles. The Iron Age people built on the natural defence of this steep scarp face; a Dobunni left a gold stater (now in Gloucester City Museum); the Romans scattered their pocket money around the 32 acres (13ha); the quarrymen dug into its defences for stone to build Uley village ½ mile (.8km) away, and arable farmers have ploughed up the earthworks, but one can still make a spectacular promenade around its perimeter.

To make the detour, hug close to the B4066 on top of Crawley Hill, just south of the barns. The immediate area is full of tempting byways to explore while, eastward, Dingle Wood curves seductively to the secluded gem Owlpen. An exquisite clutch of church, mill, manor with a gazebo in the garden and a cider press in the barn, of all ages and all of Cotswold stone so all of a piece, there is a Brigadoon-like quality about Owlpen that makes it like no other place I know, especially if you come upon it as I did following the instructions of old Ferribee, a long-ago landlord from Uley: 'First you go down Fiery Lane to Cuckoo Brook, on to Horn Knep to go round by Dragon's Den; carry on to Potlid Green and so to Marling's End. Kip straight on to Olepen, but take care not to miss the road.'

*Cam Long Down from Hodgecombe Farm*

Easier to find is Uley, nestling under the neck of the hillfort. A long street-village, Uley was famous for its blue broadcloth. Uley blue and Stroud scarlet were worn with pride by those who fought in the Napoleonic Wars, and by the military ever since. As the streams of each valley were employed in the cloth-making industry, the dyeing had to be done in other areas, therefore the blue waters of Uley were a product of the industrial era rather than any romantic connotation. The heritage stands today as a fine collection of clothiers' houses, the hipped stone roofs being typical of the village rather than of the region. The church is on a spectacular site, high up on a bank with a good view of the valley.

The Cotswold Way leaves these hill-top diversions to loop north-westward through the wood down to Hodgecombe Farm and then, following the access track, stiled pastureland ascends to a stile at the tree-fringed easterly edge of Cam Long Down.

# 13

# Cam Long Down to Stinchcombe Hill

On the southerly slopes of Cam Long Down can still be seen the strip lynchets which the Angles introduced into the farming landscape. By cutting terraces into the hillsides the steeper gradients were easier to cultivate; they also conserved the rainwater.

Cam Long Down, curiously formed as a geological outlier hill, is as all old Cotsallers know, the final feat, and defeat, of the Devil. All along the Way we have tracked him; from his Chimney at Leckhampton, his table at Crickley, to the yews at Painswick, he has been a constant challenge. It was the proliferation of churches in the Cotswolds, as well as the Holy Grail at Hailes, that gave rise to the saying 'as sure as God's in Gloucestershire', and that, of course, made Old Nick hopping mad. So, determined to flood the Cotswolds and rid it of the Deity, the Devil started to pull down the escarpment in order to use the stones to dam the Severn below. As he made his way laden from the hills he came across a local cobbler, a string of holey shoes around his neck. The Devil asked how far it was to the Severn. Suspicious of the wily old character, the cobbler pointed to the string of shoes and said he had worn them all out on his journey from the river. It was a hot day and quarrying had already tired Old Nick, so he

*View from the top of Cam Long Down*

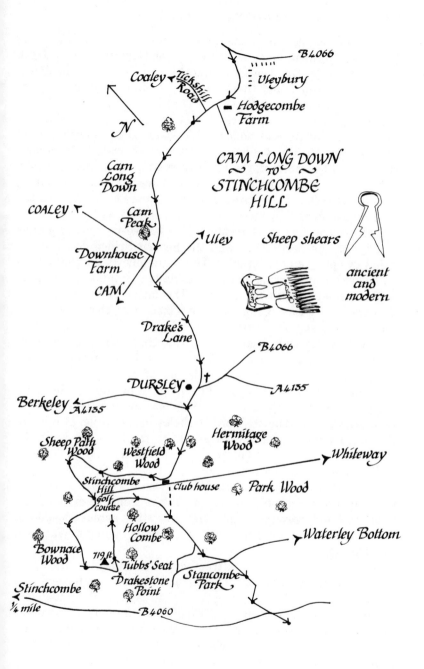

B4066

Coaley ◄ Tickshill Road

Uleybury

Hodgecombe Farm

CAM LONG DOWN
~ TO ~
STINCHCOMBE
HILL

N

Cam Long Down

COALEY ◄

Cam Peak

Uley

Sheep shears

ancient and modern

Downhouse Farm

CAM ◄

Drake's Lane

B4066

DURSLEY ●

A4135

Berkeley ◄
A4135

Hermitage Wood

Sheep Path Wood

Westfield Wood

Whiteway

Stinchcombe Hill Golf course

Club house

Park Wood

Hollow Combe

Waterley Bottom

Bownace Wood

719 ft. ▲ Tubbs' Seat

Drakestone Point

Stancombe Park

Stinchcombe ◄
¼ mile

B4060

abandoned his idea and tipped the stones out – thus Cam Long Down was formed. Now he skulks in the Severn clays by Hock Cliff judging by the 'Devil's toenails' found there. Our medieval forefathers even found them useful – ground down and mixed with whey they made a fine cattle cure-all!

The top of the Down, looking flat from a distance, is full of humps and tuffets and hollows. We watched the morning mist wreathing over the valley below while we walked in bronze sunlight on the summit, the bracken rusting at our feet already. It was like being suspended in a time warp. Then the baring topmost branches of the trees stretched upwards and pushed the mist away; farms, hedges and fields emerged and a motorway pulled toy cars across the valley. The Malverns were a mauve smudge to the north-west, and the Severn Bridge down in the valley swept away into infinity. The route follows the contours of the Down's ridge, arcing along the table-land from east to west to descend steeply from Cam Peak. The latter is the Cotswolds' Calvary, where Easter-tide wayfarers meet up with pilgrims from Cam and Dursley to celebrate the Passion.

The Way descends steeply to a stile, then left to Downhouse Farm. The minor road leads to Cam where the superfine cloth for the papal robes is still made in this, one of the only two working cloth mills of these valleys. The village grew up on the cloth trade, symbolised by sheep's heads on the buttresses of St George's Church. Thomas Lord Berkeley, in expiation of Edward II's murder at Berkeley Castle a little to the west, built the church at Upper about 1340; the vicar designed St Bartholomew's at Lower five hundred years later.

The route continues opposite Downhouse Farm, across pasture to a stile on the corner, and on to Drake's Lane; then along the field headland, through a gate and over stiles across a paddock, descending by way of Chestal Steps, cut out by fellow Wardens, into Dursley.

Dursley, sheltered in an attractive position between the spurs of Cam Peak and Stinchcombe Hill, was already established as a manor of some worth at Domesday. Of the castle built by Roger de Berkeley, a Norman with royal English blood, no trace remains, and, having weathered the tempestuous times of Stephen and Matilda and shared in the vicissitudes of the Berkeley family for centuries, the town sought some semblance of independence by entering in the medieval wool trade.

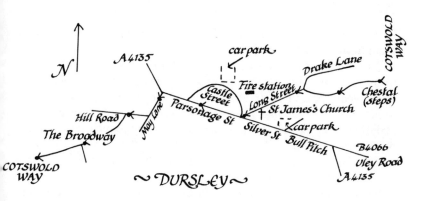

The importance of Dursley as a major cloth-making centre is said to have hinged on an immigrant Dutch weaver whose family was persuaded to take advantage of the good living promised by the king and council, who implied that at the time the English knew no more what to do with their wool than the sheep that wore it. The Dutch craftsmen seized the opportunity to lift their status even further from artisan to master by marrying into rich English families – a match encouraged by those astute enough to see how profits doubled from fleece to fabric.

Whether Dursley folks could not get their tongues round the Dutch weaver's name, or whether he wanted a more socially acceptable one, or whether a titulary honour was accorded him for his part in their prominence of the industry, we shall perhaps never know; but Webb he became, named after the Old English *webb* (weave) which he taught so successfully to the townsfolk. The Priory, at the bottom of the hill from Long Street, was built for the Webbs in 1539 and points to the standing of the family at that time, though it is distinguished more for its endurance than its architecture.

Divorcing oneself from the once-famed 'woolly' past is called development in Dursley. Nothing has been done to perpetuate it, in fact to call someone 'a man o' Dursley' is still understood locally as questioning his integrity. The term dates back half a millennium to the shady practice of some Dursley clothiers of selling their cloth folded in such a way as to hide patches of inferior dyeing or weaving, or short measure. An Act of Parliament stopped this trick, but the 'men of Dursley' then took to stretching the cloth to increase the yardage and to thickening it by fulling-in 'flock'. So infamous did the practice become that

Bishop Latimer in the sixteenth century condemned it in an open sermon as 'filling with devil's dust'.

Whatever other devices the clothiers practised were well protected by the strict indentures drawn up between the broadweavers and their apprentices. One dated 1743 bound the apprentice for 42s 'his Master's secrets to keep', together with prohibition of entering into matrimony or frequenting ale-houses or playing dice for the eight-year term. The masters did not always honour their contracts with their hard-worked employees and sometimes payment took the form of truck. One weaver who got his employer convicted in 1755 declared that, for the cloth which had taken him a fortnight to weave in his own cottage, he received 'bread, flour, bacon and shoose [sic]' and only 2s of the 28s owing to him; with rent at 3s 11d and candles for light costing 9d, he was in despair. Parish relief applications in 1798 had to attest the sobriety of the husband; by this time the local lampoonists' doggerel included 'drunken Dursley' as well as 'strutting Stroud and Painswick proud'.

Riots and strikes, petitions and bankruptcies, spread over the nineteenth century; and although localised and short-lived, their effects were far-reaching and long lasting. Poor relief was strictly poor relief, there were too many poor and no prosperity to support them. Entire communities crumbled as families emigrated rather than face the grim alternative of the workhouse. Veiled in Victorian euphemism as the 'house of industry', the workhouse rules were forbidding even by the standards of the day. All goods were to be handed in on admission, cleaned and used for the service of the House; those who missed church forfeited the next meal; no one was allowed beyond the prescribed bounds without a ticket from the governor; all exceeding the free time permitted were to be 'double the time they exceed in the Dungeon and forfeit the next meal'; all to be kept at work from 6am to 8pm; all 'idle or pretend Ailments to be kept on bread and water till willing to work in the Dungeon'.

Sixty-eight persons from 'beggarly Bisley' joined the great exodus of Stroud Valley weavers to America and Australia in 1837. Thus when Don Downton, a fellow Cotswold Warden, reported that an Australian lady on his guided walk of this area was from Adelaide's Uleybury, named by the original settlers who left Uley in that poverty-stricken year, it breathed life into records stating that the expenses of persons emigrating were

£1 10s 8¾d each for clothing, plus their conveyance and the first day's provision on board the steam packet. What sadness and deep respect one feels for those families who left on the *Leyton*, clutching their 'free' Bibles and prayer books in their hands and nursing love for their native Cotswolds in their hearts as they sailed away from Bristol dock that hot August day.

It is ironic that within a mere five years of that big step that took them halfway across the world from the wooded valleys they loved, the depression that had taken some two centuries to sink into was lifted, not through any regeneration of the old wool industry, but because of an expansion throughout the Stroud Valley of its ancillary trades. A tripartite pattern evolved. Subsidiary and complementary to the wool trade was silk weaving, the manufacturing of chemical dyes in place of growing and harvesting natural plants, carpet making, the use of textile waste for paper and flocks and shoddy, and fibreboard – most of the country's feet have walked on Cotswold-made fibreboard insoles in their shoes; millwrighting woodworkers turned their turnery skills to all kinds of woodware from walking sticks to pianos; and mill smiths turned their foundry skills to all kinds of metalworking. By 1911 only four woollen manufacturers were listed in the Stroud Valley. But though the industries changed, the valley still stuck to the power it knew best to drive its mill wheels; where forty-five mills were still using water, only eight had converted to steam, with a hesitant eighteen using both steam and water.

Foundry workers became engineers and, of the new industries, Lister's is the success story of the century. Robert Ashton Lister was born in Dursley, his father, it is said, having literally walked into the wool trade there from Yorkshire. After a time in his father's business making wire brushes to card the wool ready for spinning, Robert set up his own firm of R.A. Lister & Company in 1867, with a staff of one man and a boy. Expanding his engineering skills to making agricultural machinery, by 1907 the firm was reported to be the best in the world for churns, cooperage goods and kindred products.

Today, Lister's is the largest employer in and around the Cotswolds. And in the strange way that the threads of history tie together the ages, Lister's now has its offices in The Priory which was built for the Webb family – the Flemish weavers who founded the wool industry in Dursley. A religious house from the days of

Queen Anne, hence its name, The Priory is said to be haunted and local legend says there is a secret passage linking it with the parish church. Its Tudor origins endow Lister's offices with fine oak panelling. Its elegant Edwardian garden parties, however, are now replaced by more comprehensive gatherings. When the 'old firm', as it is affectionately known, celebrated its centenary, some 10,000 people joined in the jubilations in the town's recreation ground; the climax to the occasion being royal recognition in the Queen's Award to Industry. Side by side with all its new technology into expanding export markets, Lister's still holds a special place in the local way of life, and has just perfected a new range of Golden sheep shears. All may change around us, but sheep's wool changes not at all, only the speed and ease with which it can be parted from the sheep.

The Cotswold Way enters Dursley by the way of Long Street, distinguished by its mainly eighteenth-century buildings amid which the Old Bell accommodates the ghost of 'a tragic chamber-maid' who is reputed to have called to guests that it was 8 o'clock – at 3 in the morning.

The church of St James stands on the corner behind a neatly grassed apron. It does not conform to the usual wool-church style, despite being built in the 1450s. It had a spire, although they were going out of fashion a century before, but this was deemed unsafe in 1698. Some 2½ tons of lead were used in its extensive repairs, and to celebrate the completion of the work the bells rang heartily from the tower on 7 January 1699 – and brought the spire down!

This 'casualty and great Mischance' cost the lives of several bystanders and much of the medieval tower. The estimate for repairs was given as £1,995 0s 9d, far beyond the means of the town, so a petition was made to William III for permission to have an appeal read in churches throughout the kingdom. The brief was not granted until Anne was on the throne. Donations totalled £569 13s 9d, of which the tower builders spent 5s 3d for 'beere at ye Bell' before they started work. On completion of the tower and new bell there was 5s 9d in hand, certainly not enough to aspire to a spire. Neighbouring towns murmured that the town was now better off than if the disaster had never occurred, and that the reason why the statue of Queen Anne was stood up on the Market House was because it was she who helped them build the tower on the cheap; for when the subscribers' list was examined (they say) not a single parishioner of Dursley had subscribed a single penny!

The Market House, topped with a small bell turret, stands sentinel in the middle of the road where the Way leads westward along shop-lined Parsonage Street then left into May Lane. Veering right into Hill Road leads up The Broadway and steeply up the wooded scarp to Stinchcombe Hill, a beech-clad bastion, cleft deeply with secretive lanes and enchanting combes, glimpsed briefly by us through baring trees on climbing the headland. The B4060 runs round its bulk at 400ft (122m) bringing golfers to play on its celebrated course 300ft (91m) higher. A more idyllic setting is hard to find, although the first-time golfer may be disadvantaged by half the holes being blind from the tee. The hill is a vaguely clover-leaf shape, and a short cut across its 'stem' runs from the club house in a direct line to the westerly edge, aiming roughly at the second tee. But wayfarers interested in the scenic delights will skirt the 2 mile (3.2m) edge of the course, walking anti-clockwise, therefore in an opposite direction to the progression of the golfers. Westfield Wood edges the first 'leaf', and Sheep Path Wood the second, with a fine view over Dursley. At the tenth tee on the scarp edge the drone of the motorway rises from the valley, but it is worth suffering the sounds for the sights. Due west is the impressive bulk of Berkeley Castle where Edward II was murdered and the Berkeley family has lived for eight hundred years, making it the oldest inhabited house in Gloucestershire; it was the last Royalist stronghold in the Civil War. Beyond, are the nuclear power stations of Berkeley and Oldbury – seen by us as square and sober against setting sun-silvered clouds. The Severn Bridge touches the shoulder of the Forest of Dean, darkly distant next to tree-fringed May Hill. The Sugar Loaf and Skirrid Fawr of Wales can be seen on a clear day. An arrowhead of wild geese honked over our heads, giving warning of their approach to Sir Peter Scott's Slimbridge sanctuary only 4 miles (6.4km) away, and possibly stopping over for bed and breakfast. With over 1,800 different species of migratory and resident birds in his spacious Severn estuarine grounds, the famous explorer's son has the largest collection of wildfowl in the world. In the distant north-east is the last glimpse of the Malverns whose misty mauve shadow has been our travelling companion for so long.

Peace and tranquillity is swiftly restored as you move away from the edge, the traffic noise gobbled up by the wooded hill.

Above Brownace Wood, roughly at the ninth tee, the eye ranges over eleven counties. Sheltering below is the little village of Stinchcombe, home to the famous tractarian Isaac Williams and the novelist Evelyn Waugh. A seat and shelter commemorating Sir Stanley Tubbs who gave the hill and woods to the public are just above Drakestone Point, where a fabled dragon once stood guardian of these hills. More recent guardians were the Home Guards, alerted and to the ready at the report of paratroopers landing in Dursley; but their training was not put to the test as the message was misheard and the invasion was actually in Jersey! True to neighbouring town rivalry, this story is spread abroad at Tetbury, who did have a bomb which scattered poor old Moonlight, a cow, all over the town. Following the curve of the third 'leaf' of Stinchcombe Hill, the view above Hollow Combe is superb, and to the south pinpointing the prominent landmarks of the Tyndale and Somerset monuments, with Hanging Hill beyond.

After the promenade around the great promontory, a path to the right leads through the wood down to a watery hollow and ascends over stiles to a minor road. The road leads down to the Bottoms — Tyley, Ozleworth and Waterley; just clutches of cottage, pub and farm among cattle-grazed pastures and sloping sheep-walks, in deep cleft bottoms. Wildflower-edged paths lead a crazed course from one to another, the wind laughs in the high tree-tops above your head and all the birds of the countryside chirp and chortle, call and carol in their secure world. From the depths of Waterley Bottom come the mummers. Having had the Devil bedevil the Cotswold edge for so long we nurture a kind of love-hate relationship, so every Christmas the old adversary is hauled out for an airing and given what for by the hero of the day. The Waterley Bottomers, who helped me resurrect the ancient tradition, 'put paid' to a fearsome dragon through the doughtiness of a virile St George in front of Dursley church — and on a Cotswold pub-crawl until New Year. I favour old Beelzebub 'cos he's in our church window leering down on us with 'is yellow heyes and white tith'.

# 14

# Stinchcombe Hill
# to Wotton-under-Edge

From Stinchcombe Hill, the Way skirts Stancombe Park with its romantic garden set down in the valley far below the house. Landscape artists speak derisively of the design, but on the rare occasions in midsummer when it is opened I savour the romance of the rose-scented garden with its moss-cushioned cascades, grottoes and tunnelled tracks, for here one might chance upon the ghosts of the naughty Nibley vicar and his gipsy lover, for whom he had the secret garden laid out beyond the sight of his wife in her Georgian style house above. North Nibley is but a short walk away. At the end of Lower House Lane, the church where the wayward reverend preached is a little to the right. Corbels with king-posts supporting the magnificent nave roof and the beautiful gold-mosaic reredos catch the eye. Grace Smith, accorded the colourful effigy, was the wife of John Smyth, historian of the Berkeley family.

Upholding the powerful Berkeley line made history on Nibley Green below the church. The last pitched battle between private armies was fought here in 1470 to settle the issue of rightful inheritance to the considerable Berkeley estates and fortune. Legal wrangling and illegal villainy on both sides having failed to bring the title of right to a satisfactory settlement, Thomas Talbot, Lord Lisle – a grandson of the Countess of Warwick and Lord of Painswick Manor – challenged Lord William Berkeley, who had succeeded to the title and lands of his childless uncle, Lord Thomas (whose memorial can be seen in Wotton-under-Edge church). Taking up the challenge, Lord Berkeley replied that he would not bring a tenth of the force at his command but 'will appoint a short day to ease thy malicious heart and thy false counsell that is with thee, fail not tomorrow to be at Niblyes Green at eight or nine of the clock and I will not fail . . . to meet thee at the same place'. Each side duly turned up on 20 March with about a thousand retainers. The 20-year-old Lord Lisle, with

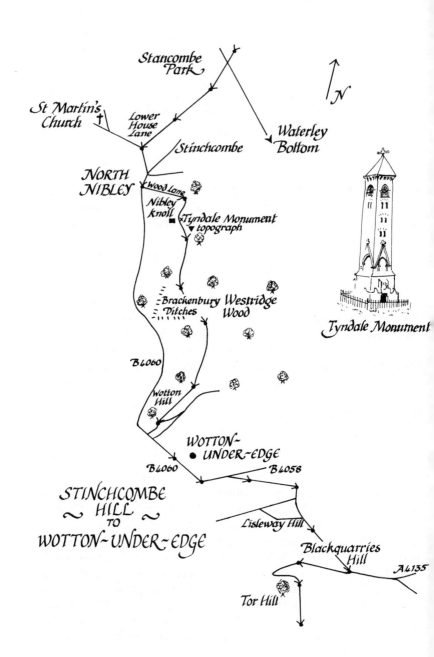

Stancombe
Park

St Martin's
Church

Lower
House
Lane

Stinchcombe

Waterley
Bottom

N

NORTH
NIBLEY

Wood Lane

Nibley
Knoll

Tyndale Monument
topograph

Brackenbury Westridge
Ditches        Wood

B4060

Wotton
Hill

WOTTON~
UNDER~EDGE

B4060

B4058

STINCHCOMBE
~ HILL ~
TO
WOTTON~UNDER~EDGE

Lisleway Hill

Blackquarries
Hill

A4135

Tor Hill

Tyndale Monument

*North Nibley church*

the hot blood and inexperience of youth, led his men into what the records regard as an ambush, and was shot 'as his beaver (visor) was up' by one Black Will, a forester. The bloody conflict was totally ineffective in determining the true Berkeley heir.

Feudal and political squabbles crossed North Nibley's threshold more than once. Seeking independence from their fickle masters in the seventeenth century, the villagers built 'six distinct habitations with chimnies in them' with their own hands in stone, timber and thatch which they quarried and foraged themselves to house their poor and infirm neighbours – but on church land. Legal wranglings followed, but the jury agreed to let the almshouses stay in view of the destitute condition of the villagers who lived by their children's 'pillfering and stealing in every corner'. Nothing remains today of those unhappy dwellings and the battle site is totally unmarked.

The monument that dominates the ridgeway is to William Tyndale, who suffered martyrdom in 1536 for his translation of the Bible causing 'the New Testament to be printed in the mother tongue of his countrymen'. The 111ft (34m) high tower was built by public subscription at a cost of £1,550 in 1886 but, exposed to the severest of the weather, it is in need of major restoration. The Tyndale Monument Charity was first set up in 1924 to keep this focal point on the landscape properly maintained; today it is estimated that £25,000 is needed to save it, exactly the same sum as quoted for restoring the Devil's Chimney which we walked past at Leckhampton. It will be interesting to see which is deemed the more worthy of salvation – the architecturally designed memorial of Victorian piety, or the curiously quarried monument of Georgian idiosyncrasy. A notice board at Wood Lane gives details of access to the tower. Follow the waymarks to reach the plateau of Nibley Knoll. A topograph gives identity to the patchwork of Berkeley Vale.

We hastened our step as fast-scudding clouds banked ominously and, not for the first time, complimented Ted Fryer, our Head Warden, for his sensible preference for walking the Way from south to north thereby keeping the prevailing south-westerly at his back. The Knoll tapers off into the welcome shelter of Westridge Wood, where yet another hillfort clings to the scarp slope. Brackenbury Ditches is triangular in shape and tranquil in its seclusion, partly obscured as it is in mature woodland. Beech-mast made attractive patterns against the stormy sky and we picked a handful of rose hips, thinking how the June roses must have enchanted earlier Cotswold Wayfarers.

As the Way approaches Wotton Hill, echoes of more barbaric times linger in the isolated spot where cocks were pitted one against the other for the sport and spoils of the townsmen. The trees in the walled plantation were first planted in 1815 to commemorate Waterloo, but were later felled for a victory bonfire to celebrate the end of the Crimean War; replanting took place to mark Queen Victoria's Golden Jubilee. A steep descent, aided by hand rails, leads to the B4060, keeping left to enter Wotton.

Wotton, backed by the steep wooded cliffs of the escarpment, is a physical punctuation mark in the story of Cotswold, looking as it does to the gentler southern slopes. Like its neighbouring town of Dursley, Wotton has made the transition from its wool-trading past to develop an identity of its own in a modern age. Again, like Dursley, it was part and parcel of the Berkeley Estate; but it retained its allegiance to, and dependence on, the Berkeleys for much longer.

The Saxon wooded farm *Wudu tun*, which comes down to us as Wotton, is further identified in its position under the Cotswold edge. The Cotsaller's habit of telescoping syllables to draw out the vowels has made the local pronunciation sound like Wuttunundredge to those 'oo don't speak as we'. The then village was put to the torch by King John's mercenaries when they devastated the Berkeley lands in reprisal for the part the second Robert Lord Berkeley played in the barons' revolt. The original church must have been destroyed at that time. The might of the

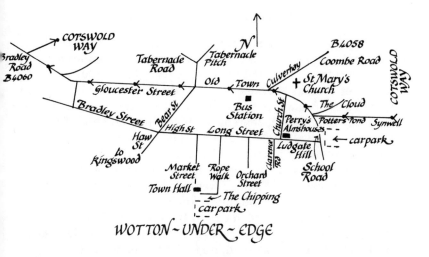

WOTTON ~ UNDER ~ EDGE

Berkeleys gave rise to the simile, 'he thinks himself as great as my Lord Berkeley'. It was no idle boast either that the Berkeleys could once hunt across the Cotswolds through the woods of Oxfordshire and into London's Hyde Park with the oldest (at least in name) Hunt in England.

The town was rebuilt after the fire and gained considerably in status when Thomas, Lord Berkeley, chose to build his manor house on the east side of the church during one of the many family feuds in which one or other of the Berkeleys were banned from the castle, a short distance away in the vale below. His is the only Berkeley memorial in the church. Grandson of the Thomas who was implicated in the murder of Edward II, he is shown with his wife Margaret in a pair of brasses considered to be one of the earliest and finest in this memorial-brass-rich county.

Betrothed at the age of fourteen to the seven-year-old Margaret, their arranged marriage, as evidenced by what Thomas himself had inscribed on the tomb:

> In youth our parents joyn'd our hands, our selves, our hearts,
> This tombe our bodyes hath, th'heavens our better parts.

was evidently a happy one, but it tragically sparked off the reason for the battle at Nibley Green. Lady Margaret died at the age of thirty. Their only child, Elizabeth, married Richard Neville, Earl of Warwick. With no direct male heir to claim the inheritance, the family's loss of succession kept them at each other's throats for some two hundred years, during which time Wotton Manor came under attack several times. Ironically, the young Lord Lisle – claimant to the Berkeley lands – had made the Manor his home and it was from there that he set off in 1470 to meet his fate at the hands of 'cousin' Berkeley. After the battle, Berkeley's men sacked Lisle Manor, as it was then called, the young Lady Lisle promptly miscarrying thereby 'extinguishing all hope of continuance of the (rival) male line'. The Manor was still in ruins when Leland, antiquary to Henry VIII, visited Wotton in 1530.

Leland also noted that the town was well occupied by clothiers, but records speak of Flemish weavers here at least two hundred years earlier. By the time the reckoning was taken of all men fit and able to take up arms for Lord Berkeley in 1608, over half of Wotton's inhabitants were engaged in the cloth trade. Ancient feudal ties had been severed, and a living made at the loom and wheel; mercers, merchants and mill owners were the new masters, not the manor. But the manorial system, with all its faults, was long established and exercised a pastoral interest in those who were tied to it in servitude and attracted the avid attention of those who were not, as revealed in a letter from a local guest at the coming-of-age party of Lord Dursley at Berkeley Castle in 1807:

> . . . this grand event is over. The number of people was guessed at about 200, the guests staying at the Castle were by no means numerous and only four ladies among them . . . Lady C wore the greatest profusion of diamonds and pearls I ever saw and seemed to have been puzzled how to find space to hand and stick them all about her . . . The Duke and Lady Berkeley led the way to supper . . . very elegant but much more for show than use. There were eatables enough but so adorned and disguised that it was very difficult to find out what they were and when the useful discovery was made it was ten to one whether a knife and fork could be got at to cut them up.

The new bosses could not compare with this standard, but aspired to seek the status of 'gentlemen' clothiers, though with few philanthropic leanings. One of the exceptional few was Hugh Perry who remembered his birthplace when he was rich and famous in London, having made his fortune as a mercer and his fame as city sheriff. His endowments were practical as well as pious: a conduit gave Wotton its first water supply; his almshouses a legacy of Cotswold architecture at its domestic best, with its own chapel in the courtyard in the seventeenth century. Thomas Dawes, a wool broker, built a hospital opposite in 1720: both are remembered in the chapel's glowing stained-glass window, which pays pictorial tribute to the town's historic ties with the wool trade. Founding almshouses was both fashionable and functional, and Wotton is particularly well endowed with them: Ann Bearpacker left money for housing poor but regular attenders of the Church of England; nonconformists housed their poor and faithful Calvinistic followers in the shadow of the Reverend Rowland Hill's Tabernacle.

The number of almshouses and chapels reflects the independence the town sought for its kin both in body and soul in the depressed times following the closure of its numerous mills. These foundations, added to buildings of interest for their architectural merit or as houses of the town's notable sons, give Wotton character and a broader dimension of its past than a cursory glance allows. First impressions are of un-Cotsall-like colour-washing of stone-built houses, or the picking out of dripmoulds and mullions with dark paint. But take time to look behind the façade.

The way curves to the right along Bradley Street. We made a diversion left into Bear Street to go straight up the hill opposite, to Rowland Hill's Tabernacle. Many people have beaten a path to this austere grey-stone redundant chapel which dominates the Pitch to see the incredible reproduction of the famous Woodchester Roman mosaic pavement. Constructed to be portable, it is planned to exhibit it abroad. The original used to be unearthed every ten years so that we may marvel at the largest and most elaborate Romano-British mosaic north of the Alps. Laid around AD325, by craftsmen of the Corinium school of

*Woodchester Roman mosaic*

Cirencester, Britain's second largest Roman city, its condition has deteriorated so much that even the decadal excavation is deemed unwise. Brothers Bob and John Woodward of Wotton, therefore, have reproduced in meticulous detail the 2,209sq ft (205m$^2$) mosaic pavement. Exactly ten years ago I had laid the third piece of tessera in the full glare of television cameras and much publicity in what was then a well-converted, but totally bare, chapel. It was marvellous to see the complete work, and how during that decade another 1,499,997 cubes of tessera had brought Orpheus playing his lyre, and charming birds and beasts around two concentric circles, onto the floor of Wotton's old Tabernacle, while the Roman Orpheus stays safe in his underworld beneath Woodchester churchyard.

Returning down Tabernacle Pitch, Old Town, with many of its houses and old Court Manor keeping their most interesting features within their own walls, leads away to the left, then bears left to Culverhay. Here are the famous Bluecoat School, Bearpacker's Almshouses and, on the rise of Adey's Lane, the turret and bell-topped Under The Hill House where Moore Adey, the deranged friend of Oscar Wilde, searched for an imaginary treasure trove.

Retracing your steps to the top of Church Street is to be close to the route out of the town, but it would be a pity not to escape the bustle of the streets for the serenity of the quadrangle around which the Perry Almshouses and the General Hospital range like 'an Oxford college in miniature'. Church Street is the reputed site of the original grammar school founded by Katherine, Lady Berkeley, in 1384. The school has been sited at different points in the town, but still retains its name and pride in its 600-year-old history. One of its most auspicious pupils was Dr Edward Jenner, whose rustic hut-like laboratory, where he pioneered his work on smallpox vaccination, is in the grounds of Berkeley Castle.

Smallpox accounted for the tragedy in the life of Mary Perry, the daughter of Hugh who founded the almshouses. Mary married Henry Noel, of Chipping Campden Manor, and was immediately embroiled in the ravages of the Civil War. History speaks of the heroic Mary melting lead for bullets while she and her husband defended their home from the Roundheads; but their efforts failed and the newly married couple were imprisoned. It was then that Mary caught the dreaded smallpox. Her first child and husband contracted it from her and both died.

Isaac Pitman became infamous in Wotton as a teacher in the Wesleyan school – sacked from this for his religious sentiments, he joined the Church of England. He became famous for his 'system of Shorthand known as Phonography', which a plaque on his old house in Orchard Street states he invented there in 1837. As Sir Isaac he moved down the Way to the Royal Crescent in Bath.

Long Street, due west, is a busy shopping area where stands the old Tolsey, a spiked tail copper dragon weathervane on its cupola and an old cell in its cellar. Market Street is more ancient and leads down to the Chipping – our first encounter with the old name for market since we left Chipping Campden. An outer doorway, 700 years old, was hauled here from Kingswood Abbey and gives medieval character to the Victorian national school building.

The Way leads from the north side of Church Street to cross over the road to the Cloud. To the left is St Mary's Church with one of the finest towers in the Cotswolds; its famous Berkeley brasses; a tediously long epitaph to Thomas Rous, who lived at The Court from where the Berkeley loyalists hurled their abuse and refuse at Lady Warwick when she swept into town in 1421; and the organ on which Handel played. Until World War II, Wotton was one of only five places in the whole of England to observe the order of William the Conqueror's (cover fire) curfew bell at 8 o'clock every night.

# 15

# Wotton-under-Edge
# to Hawkesbury Upton

Leaving Wotton by way of Sinwell, another of Cotswolds' 'seven springs' of which the Edbrook was the first to supply water to the town, the Way follows into Coombe where a terrace of rubble-stone weavers' cottages is a reminder of the past. The old mill-stream is patterned all about with waterside plants, lush in leaf and fulsome in flower. The heights are regained by climbing steeply up Lisleway Hill and on to Blackquarries Hill. On the right a signpost points to Wortley and Alderley. Vantage viewpoints will soon be more meagre as the country moulds into softer rolling wolds, more down-like in character and contrasting sharply with the steep stature of the scarp; so the superb vista of the Vale of Berkeley with the Mendips in the distance is the more memorable.

A pair of plump pheasants see-sawed on the dry-stone wall on Tor Hill, their beautifully coloured plumage glistening jewel-like against the tall dried grasses. Their like are captured in the Woodchester mosaic, a reminder that it was the Romans who introduced these colourful birds as this 'barbarous country' had no feathered game. So, along with the Roman snail which is still occasionally found in our dry-stone walls and was once collected by children at a shilling a bucketful for the squire's table, the longwool ancestors of our Cotswold sheep to keep their legions warm, and the stinging nettle 'to warm up the British', it is no idle maxim to say 'scratch Gloucestershire to find Rome'.

Beyond the gates the track follows the contours of an ancient strip lynchet, and lying below Wortley Hill can be seen Nanny Farmer's Bottom. Wortley Hill is mainly coniferous, but the steeply banked hollow-way is a glow of primroses in the spring – already their crinkly leaves could be seen pushing through the red-brown soil. Tough stems of old man's beard twisted and tangled with neighbouring shrubs, covering everything with its wispy grey tufts. The Way has dropped some 400ft (122m) before

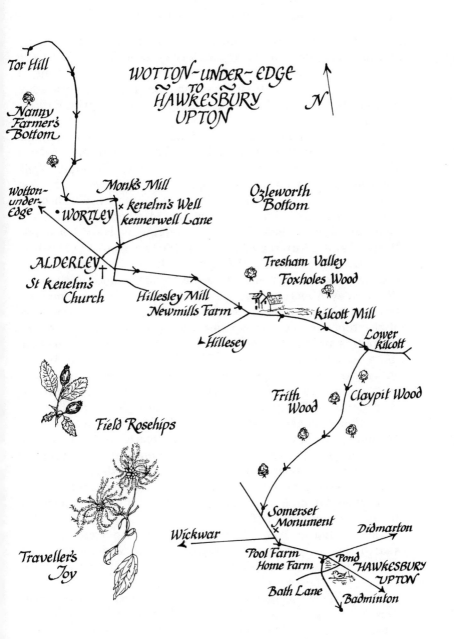

WOTTON–UNDER–EDGE
TO
HAWKESBURY
UPTON
N

Tor Hill

Nanny
Farmer's
Bottom

Wotton–
under–
Edge

Monk's Mill
×Kenelm's Well
Kennerwell Lane

• WORTLEY

Ozleworth
Bottom

ALDERLEY
St Kenelm's
Church

Hillesley Mill
Newmills Farm

Tresham Valley
Foxholes Wood

Kilcott Mill

Hillesley

Lower
Kilcott

Frith
Wood

Claypit Wood

Field Rosehips

Somerset
Monument

Wickwar

Didmarton

Tool Farm
Home Farm

Pond
HAWKESBURY
UPTON

Traveller's
Joy

Bath Lane

Badminton

it nudges tiny Wortley: the concentration of mills along its stream illustrates how every waterway was harnessed to the cloth trade. One of its sons, Stephen Hopkins, became a prosperous clothier, but left these quiet backwaters for the spice and adventure of the high seas, sailing with the Pilgrim Fathers in the *Mayflower*.

A ladder-stile marks the point where the Way goes at an angle to a stile close by Monk's Mill to cross a bridge, then veers right to Kennerwell Lane, with its sparkling spring, Kenelm's Well, overspilling from its mossy trough. Alderley is really the last Cotswold hill-village on the route. It has a link with Winchcombe through the Saxon king, St Kenelm, to whom the church is dedicated and, in local legend, the spring took on his name. Peaceful and picturesque Alderley in 1609 gave birth to Matthew Hale, Lord Chief Justice of England, who was prominent in the establishment of English law in the troubled times of the Civil War and even more restless period of the Restoration. Pious and proud in his pursuit of justice, he was also prey to the prejudices of the times, for he did not hesitate to use the sayings of the Scriptures and the 'wisdom of Parliament' in sentencing to death those accused of witchcraft. Sir Matthew is buried in the churchyard. The Grange, where he was born shortly after it was built, was later home to B. H. Hodgson who introduced the rhododendron. The garden is sometimes open to the public.

Another eminent botanist who settled in this quiet spot was Marianne North, who wrote her recollections of her life travelling the world recording and sketching rare plants, and found time to create a garden of her own at The Mount despite the ill-health her arduous expeditions left on her. In the village churchyard she is remembered in pink marble; in her garden her opossum mouse is remembered on a sundial.

The Poorhouse, now a farmhouse, recalls the Victorians who shared the poverty of their neighbouring mill villages; a barn atop staddle stones is a reminder that this is still Gloucestershire, at least for a few more yards.

On the rise of the hill past the church, the Way crosses the road to go left along a short track to a gate. In and around the old farm buildings a pretty horse and supercilious goats stood out white and elegant high up on the bank above, and an ambling grunting could have been an Old Gloucester – the ancient spotted pig, now a rare breed. There are sweeping views to the right when the

*The farm track to Tresham Valley*

trees and hedges are bare of foliage, before the path descends to the valley prior to skirting above Newmills Farm for some, usually muddy, walking. But the company of the stream takes your mind off your boots. At the stile leading to the Tresham Valley, turn right, then left, to the collective charm of Kilcott; its mill and pond are quiet and calm today belying its busy and productive past.

*Kilcott Valley*

Follow the valley road to Lower Kilcott. A right-hand, sign-posted, turn goes up a thickly hedged sunken track to the last of the large woodscaped hills. A gate from Frith Wood opens onto where the route crosses pasture land. On reaching the lane, turn left onto the road and on to Hawkesbury Monument. It is properly the Somerset Monument, erected to General Lord Robert Edward Henry Somerset, whose service under Wellington at Waterloo was commended by Parliament. Standing on the scarp face of 650ft (198m), the 144 steps up the 120ft (36m) tower gives a panoramic view of the Avon County landscape. The general was a son of the 5th Duke of Beaufort.

*Somerset monument from the lane,*
*Hawkesbury*

The family seat, some 3 miles (4.8km) to the south-east, is the celebrated home of the Badminton Horse Trials. This is Beaufort country – colloquially called 'Beaufortshire'. There is a well known sporting print of the chimney sweep at Chipping Sodbury saying 'sorry gentlemen, I can't vote for you 'cause I 'unts with the Duke'. It was General Somerset's father who turned his Hunt from the stag to the fox after chancing across one near Silk Wood about 1740.

From the tower a pavement leads on to Pool Farm with ducks on its pond. The Way turns right into Bath Lane. Hawkesbury Upton – the upper farm settlement to distinguish it from Hawkesbury in the valley below – is also a farming village. Dilapidated barns and a tiny windowless cottage swathed in old man's beard as in a cobweb are, however, sad and beggarly neighbours for Hawkesbury's rather fine church with a fireplace and chimney in its tower and the Prime Minister from the age of Waterloo in its crypt.

*View from the top of Somerset monument*

# 16

# Hawkesbury Upton to
# Old Sodbury

Just as the mill valleys behind us are of Laurie Lee's country, the softer folds of the southern wolds, at least in my mind, are of the world of Jane Austen – well, at least the sense and sensibility of the landscaped parks ahead. For the present, the countryside still belongs to us, the Wayfarers.

Wayfaring trees abounded in thorn-hedged Bath Lane. Thrushes and blackbirds worked busily on the berries while speckled starlings stripped the few remaining elderberries along this ancient trackway with its views of Severn Vale. Keeping company with Highfield Lane, the Way bears to the right at a gateway, down a field to a stile and enters the wood at the junction with Bodkin Hazel Lane, which leads off to the left to a wood of that name close by Petty France where Jane Austen's Catherine and Henry made a prolonged stop on their fictional journey from Bath to Northanger Abbey.

A descent through the wood, then down a field, brings you to Horton Court which, on account of its Norman hall, can lay claim to being the oldest inhabited house in England. The main house was built in Tudor times for Dr William Knight, the bishop who was Henry VIII's envoy to the Pope. Knight failed to get any advancement towards the king's divorce, but obviously had time enough to absorb the artistry of the Italian architecture and built the lovely ambulatory, with medallions of Roman emperors on the inner wall, to add dignity to his garden. The coat of arms above the doorway of the house includes the prothonotary hat. The house is not open to the public, but the hall and ambulatory are, at limited times.

The north wing, containing the Norman hall, is close by the church and can be glimpsed over the churchyard wall. The road leads down to the village about ½ mile (.8km) to the south. Historically, it is part of the Saxon Hundred of Grumbald's Ash –

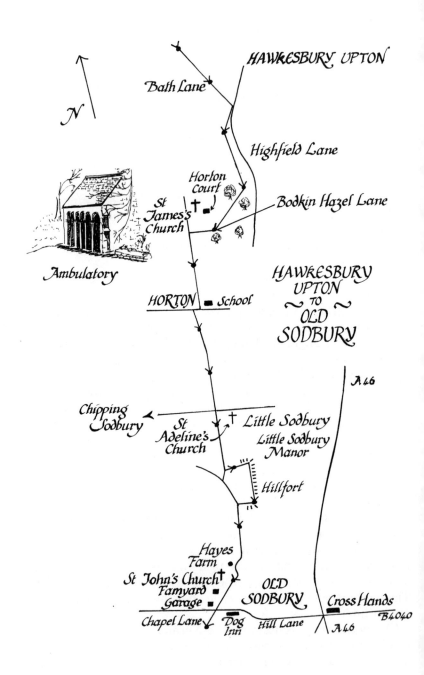

N

HAWKESBURY UPTON

Bath Lane

Highfield Lane

Horton
Court

St
James's
Church

Bodkin Hazel Lane

Ambulatory

HORTON ■ School

HAWKESBURY
UPTON
~ TO ~
OLD
SODBURY

A 46

Chipping
Sodbury

St
Adeline's
Church

† Little Sodbury

Little Sodbury
Manor

Hillfort

Hayes
Farm

St John's Church †
Famyard ■
Garage ■

OLD
SODBURY

Cross Hands

Chapel Lane

Dog
Inn

Hill Lane

A 46

B 4040

the old settlement of Grumbald's Ash seems to have disappeared under the great cross-country course of Badminton – most of the village was owned by the Duke of Beaufort. A hundred years ago, Horton was a self-sufficient little place with a post office, a bootmaker, two shops, a wheelwright who could turn his hand to general carpentry, and a blacksmith, to serve its 342 inhabitants. Victorian faith in a growing and stable community is evidenced in the school which was built for eighty children but with only one schoolmaster, aided by his wife as 'sewing mistress'. Newly built houses bear out that belief.

Right, onto the road, then left off it, takes the route from Horton across fields, past a lake to Little Sodbury by the back door as it were, the Way passing as it does between a cottage on the right and its garden. Little Sodbury is the chief contender for the birthplace of William Tyndale. Because of confusion caused by the Tyndales assuming the name of Hutchins at one period, there is scant detail of his boyhood, let alone his true place of birth. It is from his academic career at Oxford that history has gathered together the scholastic brilliance and resolute purpose that made him such a forthright advocate for reform in religious understanding. A very early manuscript from his university days was a short and sad prayer: 'Defend me, O Lord, from all them that hate me', interwoven in a drawing. Many did hate him for his relentless pursuit of his sole purpose – that of translating the Bible into English so that 'the boy that follows the plough knows more of the Bible'. The oft-quoted remark was thought to have been aimed at Dr Knight of the neighbouring village's Horton Court, who would most certainly have been one of the 'divers great-beneficed and learned men' at Sir John Walsh's table at Little Sodbury Manor.

Tyndale was tutor-chaplain to Sir John's grandsons for two years from 1522 to 1523, and preached in the original church close by. While he was at Little Sodbury Manor he worked diligently on his translation, but found eventually that 'there was no place to do it in all England'. His 'noblest monument', as he called it, was The New Testament. One vellum-bound copy was made specially for Anne Boleyn, who is known to have sympathised with the reformers. Henry VIII's royal decree that every church in England should have an English Bible was issued two years after William Tyndale had been burnt at the stake; it was three hundred years before the Cotswolds honoured her noble son and four hundred years before Westminster Abbey commemorated its exiled and martyred hero. At Sudeley, however, Katherine Parr had honoured his work contemporaneously through the services of Miles Coverdale. The rebuilt church of St Adeline dedicated, unusually, to the patron saint of Flemish weavers, has five martyrs, including Tyndale, on the pulpit panels. Of the old church only a doorway remains among the dark yew trees. Old Little Sodburians rest in peace at Old Sodbury, for they did not have a 'churchyard formed and inclosed' until 1859.

The Way passes in front of the manor and on to a farm with an ancient dew-pond system serving modern-day needs, to Sodbury Hillfort, used successively after the Iron Age by the Romans then the Saxons, who went down the Way to do battle at Dyrham. Covering 11 acres (4.4ha), it is the largest earthwork on the route. Edward IV camped his 'Roses' army here en route to the fateful battle of Tewkesbury. The herb-cushioned short sward now resounds only to the tramp of walking boots making tracks to or from Old Sodbury.

# 17

# Old Sodbury to Dyrham

Waymarks direct the route straightforwardly past Old Sodbury village school, then right to the lych-gated church, whose foundations were laid in Norman times. It contains a, now rare, wooden effigy of a knight who died six hundred years ago. From the church, the Way follows Cotswold Lane and crosses the A432 which cuts busily through to Chipping Sodbury – the Sodburys' old market centre a mile (1.6km) away to the west. The Dog Inn served the pedlars and fair-going folk in the days of Elizabeth I. This must be one of the few places where she never reputedly slept; but Elizabeth II made an enforced stop at the Cross Hands in the blizzard of Christmas 1981, after delivering family gifts to Princess Anne at Gatcombe Park. An old coaching inn, the Cross Hands owes its sign to an ancient coin, with inscription, found in the Roman encampment. The round embattled towers in the area are ducal in appearance but mundane in purpose, for they are the ventilation shafts of the railway tunnel.

Chapel Lane is followed until a gate on the left leads across gated and stiled fields to the hill road by Catchpot Cottage. Turn right on to the road and down to Coomb's End with its attractive seventeenth-century farmhouse. At a gate on the left the Way leaves the road; the stately Dodington House to the south-west is no longer open to the public, but the route skirts the 'Capability' Brown designed park, its old trees enclosing the gracious manor, shielding it from the world roaring down the M4 less than a mile (1.6km) away. The gentle and romantic landscape in which the elegant house is set is in direct contrast to the harsh conditions in which the money to build it was amassed. The Codrington family, for whom it was designed by James Wyatt, made a great fortune in the West Indies on the backs of slaves. A letter still exists of a slave seeking his freedom from Codrington, who bitterly opposed abolition. Soon after the valley footbridge is crossed, the Way passes close by our third Seven Springs – this one is the source of the River Frome. A gate at the top of the field leads to a short ascent to a narrow gate on to the A46. Cross the road with

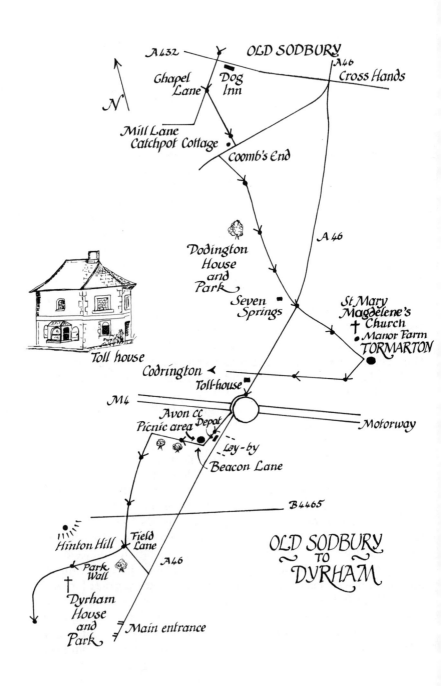

A432
OLD SODBURY
A46
Chapel
Lane
Dog
Inn
Cross Hands
N
Mill Lane
Catchpot Cottage
Coomb's End
Podington
House
and
Park
A46
Seven
Springs
St Mary
Magdelene's
Church
Manor Farm
TORMARTON
Toll house
Codrington
Toll-house
M4
Avon CC
Picnic area
Depot
Motorway
Lay-by
Beacon Lane
B4465
Hinton Hill
Field
Lane
OLD SODBURY
TO
DYRHAM
Park
Wall
A46
Dyrham
House
and
Park
Main entrance

extreme care, then stiles and fields lead on until one enters Tormarton by the Old School House.

Tormarton was on the boundary of the Saxon kingdoms of Mercia and Wessex. Recent reshuffling of shire boundaries places it in the newly formed – and hard for Gloucestershire folk to understand – Avon, where the tongue of Wiltshire licks at the village's limestone ridge of West Littleton Down, an extensive Celtic site to the south of the village. Revealed during the laying of a gasline in 1968 were the skeletons of two youths who had died a thousand years ago; flakes of the spearheads that had killed them were still embedded in their bones. The building of the M4, linking London with Bristol and South Wales, destroyed at least two Romano-British settlements as it cut along just south of the village.

Transitional work between Saxon and Norman settlement is demonstrated in the development of the church. For brass enthusiasts there is a fine fifteenth-century memorial to John Ceysill in a robe and with what looks like a pouch at his waist – depicting a civic rather than military role, although many of the old wool merchants are shown in armour. The brass is sensibly protected by a carpet, and the rector's permission is needed to make a rubbing. For those who seek the rarer features of church architecture there is wheat-ear moulding (found again only at Norwich Cathedral, according to the late David Verey) on the top Norman string-course outside the east end of the chancel. On the south side of the church is Manor Farm house, its foundations dating back to the Middle Ages. Although largely rebuilt it still retains, beside a large chimney-stack, the carved arms of John de Rivere, who founded a college of priests at Tormarton.

This is still very much Cotswold oolite stone country; the quarryland of the parish was described as 'valuable' in Victorian times. Situated as it is on the old coach road, Tormarton looked very early to Bath, and Mr Pitt the carrier ran a regular service to the city twice a week in the 1890s 'returning the same day'.

Leave the village near the Post Office, following the way-marked route crossing pastureland to a stone stile onto a footpath. Cross the complex of the motorway to follow the edge of the A46 to the second layby by the Avon CC depot, then take a right-hand turn off it to meet Beacon Lane. A picnic area is currently being developed here. Follow the wood edge to a gate, then the Way veers left to face the electricity pylons. Keeping to the edge of the fields, cross the B4465 and on to Field Lane, halting at the fork. To the right is Hinton Hill, with ancient strip lynchets on its south-easterly slopes. A Romano-British hillfort of Dyrham, history was made here in 577, for the Anglo-Saxon Chronicle records that at 'the place that is called Deorham' the Saxons Cuthwine and Ceawlin slew three kings of the Britons, gaining immediate control of Gloucester, Cirencester and Bath. The permanent result was the division between the Britons of Wales and those of the Southwest, making this one of the more decisive battles to have been fought on English soil.

The waymarked route goes to the right, descending with Dyrham Park wall to Dyrham village. National Trust members may gain access to Dyrham House through the churchyard (but have to give their names at the back door), non-members have to enter off the A46, which can be reached by turning left at Field Lane fork and right onto the A46. Dyrham village was an estate of Pershore Abbey in Saxon times, but was out of monastic control by the time of the Conquest. The hamlet of Hinton, a mile (1.6km) to the north, was included in its population – which totalled 365 in 1891, both places having a shoemaker at the time.

The church is at the end of a short lane, flanked by trees. Here the chronology of the Lords of Dyrham Manor can be traced from the thirteenth century through the memorials, starting with a superb brass of Sir Maurice and Lady Isobel Russel and an extraordinary number of funeral hatchments.

In the south aisle, close by the private entrance to the mansion – home to the Wynter family from 1571 to 1688 – is an elaborate canopied tomb to George Wynter. As Clerk of the Ships, George, and his brother who was Master of Ordnance, is said to have controlled the Elizabethan navy in a 'snug family monopoly'. George 'adventured Mr Frauncis Drake' £1100 for a voyage around the world with John Wynter, his son, as vice-admiral. John, commanding the *Elizabeth* lost contact with Drake's *Golden Hind* in the Straits of Magellan. Forced back by contrary winds, Wynter brought home with him 'Portuguese merchandise taken by Drake and his company'.

John's implication in the subsequent charge of piracy exercised all the legal skills at the command of his father. Fearing the family estate could be forfeited, George Wynter excluded John from his will unless it should later be proved 'that my eldest sonne shall be by order of lawe or otherwise therebye acquitted

and discharged from all misdemeanors of pirasies whiche is nowe
supposed against him by the Portingalls, that hathe bene
committed in the tyme while he was uppon the seas in compayne
with Frauncis Drake'. John Wynter was acquitted soon after his
father's death, and the document is preserved in the county
archives.

The Blathwayts came to Dyrham through marriage at the end
of the seventeenth century. William Blathwayt, who married
Mary Wynter, was an affluent and able civil servant, rising to
Secretary of State to William III. His salary of £2,200 in 1701
could be at least trebled in real terms by the perquisites attached
to the position. Blathwayt demolished most of the Tudor house
and rebuilt the present Dyrham House in what is regarded as an
exquisite example of baroque planning. A 'gentleman commoner',
Blathwayt was educated in the fashionable arts by his uncle
Thomas Povey, a colourful character described by Evelyn as 'a
nice contriver of all elegancies, and exceedingly formal'. But
Pepys decried him for his inefficiency in running the Tangier
Treasurership as 'the simple Povey, of all the most ridiculous
fools that I ever saw attend to business! Both diarists applauded
his 'well-contrived' cellar.

Descriptions of, and visits to, Dyrham House are well
documented, from the stiff sentences of the county historians to
the gossipy letters of his contemporaries. Blathwayt, said Sir
Robert Atkyns, 'hath a large handsome new-built house near the
church, and beautiful gardens of a great extent, with curious
water-works and pleasant walks', the Countess of Bristol wrote to
her husband that 'he [Beau Nash] and the Grantham family are
gone with two-coach fulls too day to Mr Blathwait's; I put in broad
hints for Poor Betty that had a mind to see it but they were not so

*Dyrham House*

kind to ask her to go with them'; Dudley Ryder in his diary called the house well-furnished with 'good rich beds' and described the garden as 'most pleasant situated upon several hills that entertain the eyes with a variety of prospects . . . there is a cascade from a very steep hill of 224 steps, the finest in England except for the Duke of Devonshire's. At one side of the garden there is a wilderness of high trees in which there are many agreeable shades. In one of them we made our dinner of some cold things . . . we gave the gardener 5s. and the woman that showed the house the same'.

In the spacious park where horse-riders weaved between newly planted trees we too 'made our dinner', adding iron and crunch to our hunks of bread and cheese with a lovely bunch of watercress we had picked fresh from the stream a little way back – a delight which would have been denied us had we chanced upon it in midsummer, for we still live by country lore and would not eat watercress or game if there is no 'R' in the month! We also bade greeting to the magpie which crossed our path. We were not so sure as to how the delightful fallow deer should be greeted. We came upon them suddenly and they completed the scene; the very name of the house is *deor hamm*, meaning deer enclosure, and Dyrham has had deer in its grounds for over a thousand years. The boundary wall is Cotswold dry-stone with combers – a feature which is fast disappearing from our countryside as stone gets more expensive to quarry, wallers more scarce and con-creters insensitive to congruity and tradition.

The major historic interest of Dyrham House, set deep in the fold of the hills, is that it reflects the domestic taste of the last decade of the seventeenth century, the original arrangements of the furnishings having been reconstructed from the house-keeper's inventories. There are many things to delight many people. There is a fine collection of pictures, including those in the great central Tudor hall which, after Fonthill was sold in 1805, had been built into the ceiling of Bath's Theatre Royal. There they became darkened by smoke, so were sold to Colonel Blathwayt, thereby escaping the fire that destroyed the theatre in 1862. Furniture, firearms and furnishings include a crimson and yellow velvet-covered State Bed, bought for the 'Best Bed Chamber above Stairs' in case Queen Anne happened to come – which proved more improbable as Blathwayt gradually lost favour with the fourth of the monarchs he served; muskets to

defend the house against marauders; and walnut and cedar, inset
with damask, panelling in the closet – the little room furnished
for reading and privacy as part of the 'politer way of living'
introduced by Charles II. All a far cry from the house from which
Wynter sailed forth with Drake, for then even the 'greate
chamber' had only a walnut bedstead, a lesser bed and a livery
cupboard with 'one wallnutt tree chayre broken and two cussions
rott eaten' stored elsewhere.

Students of architecture will liken the style of Dyrham to a
town house of its period and point out continental overtones in
the façade; avid horticulturists will mourn the passing of the
formal gardens to become extensive parkland; and delftware
devotees will pore over the pyramid flower vases and jardinières.
For those like me who seek pleasure in simpler things, there are
the embroidered aprons which fashionable ladies wore over their
dresses until banned at the Bath assemblies by Beau Nash. Jane
Austen fans can compare the visit of Humphry Repton to Dyrham
in 1800 when he was paid £66 3s, although Jane Austen in
*Mansfield Park* gives his fees as 5 guineas a day, but travelling
expenses were additional. For many war-wounded there will be
the memory of hospital beds in half the house; and as a memorial
to those who did not survive World War II, Dyrham House and
Park were acquired by the National Trust for all to enjoy.

# 18
# Dyrham to Hanging Hill

The Way leaves Dyrham downhill and turns southwards through Sands Farm. The cultivated field which follows leads, through a gap, onto the headland of the next. Pasture land takes the track down to a plank footbridge; then ascends to the skeletal remains of an old woodland where once there were coppice craftsmen cleaving and weaving wattles for the shepherd's cot, splitting spars and pics for thatcher's pegs, selecting pea and bean sticks for the cottager's garden and bundling up the brash for the local baker's bread ovens. The stream bed adds character, as do the stiled gates.

On leaving the wood, a track across pasture land comes onto a byroad which follows the ancient Jurassic Way atop the limestone backbone running from Bath to the Humber. After a short distance, turn left onto the narrow road, then right through a gate, to follow the hedgeline to a lane leading into Pennsylvania – a little straggle of a place, about as un-Cotswold as its name. Crossing the busy A46, look for a stile on the left that leads across two cultivated fields at an angle; a gate then opens onto a pavement alongside the A40. Turning left, go to the White Hart public house which, it announces on the side, was built circa 1600. Cross over directly opposite, to the bus-stop sign on the Cotswold Way post.

This is Cold Ashton, and it *was* cold. From this approach there is no immediate feeling of elevation, but it is 700ft (213m) up. As I stopped to sketch the lovely old iron kissing-gate cuddled close to the stone wall, the first snows of winter fell – or rather they hurled straight across the plateau from the Bristol Channel. The high stone wall on the right provided a 'bit of burra' to the fine chestnut, beech and hawthorn, but none to us Wayfarers in a blizzard. In warmer times the grassy walk, keeping boots off the crops that verge to its edge, must be a delight. Kissing gates are certainly popular at Cold Ashton; the churchyard has one at each end. The design remains the same – I wonder if there is a standard English kiss!

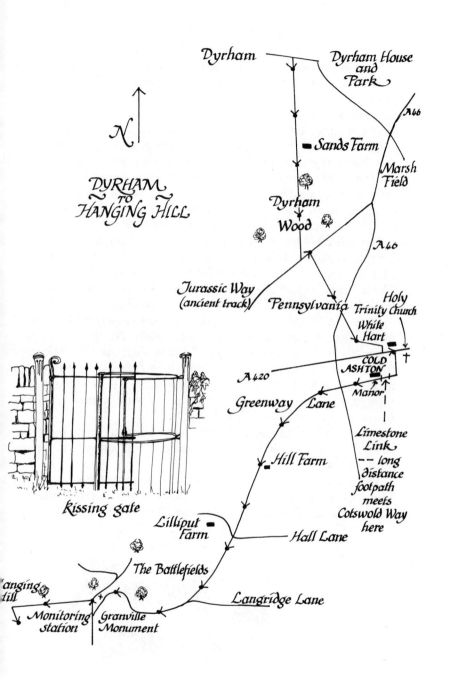

# DYRHAM TO HANGING HILL

N

Dyrham

Dyrham House and Park

A46

Sands Farm

Marsh Field

Dyrham Wood

A46

Jurassic Way (ancient track)

Pennsylvania

Holy Trinity Church

White Hart

A 420

COLD ASHTON

Manor

Greenway Lane

Limestone Link

-- long distance footpath meets Cotswold Way here

Hill Farm

Kissing gate

Lilliput Farm

Hall Lane

The Battlefields

anging ill

Langridge Lane

Monitoring station

Granville Monument

The churchyard has a particularly quieting effect. It is not exactly neglected, but neither is it manicured. There was no sign of recent flowers, just yew and laurel spreading huge swags of greenery over a number of graves. Moss and ivy welded headstone and table-tomb together and, standing close to one whose sculpted lilies in a rondel were as crisp as if cut yesterday, with a little shiver I noticed it was to a family of my name! Inside the church there are memorials to the Whittingtons, and near the church is Whittington Farmhouse. The oak-panelled pulpit set into the wall on the stairs of the former roodloft has the most exquisite stone canopy with crockets and pinnacles like a fairy castle; it is said that Bishop Latimer preached from it.

The villagers have obviously always cared for their lovely old church: a hundred years ago it was reseated and refloored for £1,100, raised by subscription from a population of a mere 344. There are beautifully worked wool-tapestry hassocks commemorating the Silver Jubilee of 1977 – so the caring continues.

Priests of the parish must have been particularly well endowed in the past, for the main rebuilding of Holy Trinity was carried out in Tudor times by the rector, Thomas Key; the school close by the church was built in the Gothic style in 1860 by the rector as a memorial to his brother, J. Sayre. The school is now closed, the rope from the bell secured to the wall of what is now a private house, a sad reminder of times past.

At the end of the short church walk the route turns right. On the left-hand side St Catherine's valley falls away into sheep-studded folds.

The marker on the gatepost signals the start of the Limestone Link walk, brainchild of my fellow warden, Cyril Trenfield. Running from Cold Ashton through St Catherine's Valley and

*St Catherine's Valley, Cold Ashton*

Stoke Valley, then alongside the Kennet and Avon Canal and on to the north scarp of the Mendips to Shipham just inside the Somerset boundary, the forty-two mile route links the Cotswold Way with the West Mendips Way. It has been cleared by the Bristol and Avon Area Ramblers Association who together with the Avon District Cotswold Wardens are now waymarking it.

The best view of Cold Ashton manor house is from the top of the first field for then the perfect scale and symmetry of the Elizabethan building can be appreciated. From the lane itself it is the Renaissance gateway which commands attention. The rectory makes a fitting architectural neighbour. Sir Bevil Granville returned here to die of his wounds following the battle of Lansdown in 1643; a monument to his valour is the next landmark on route.

Descending to the busy A46, the Way crosses the road into Greenway Lane; the grass track lies under the tarmac, but the valley it drops into is still green. Hamswell House standing four-square to the west was once home to a branch of Dick Whittington's family: the Hamswell Estate charity was the major support of Cold Ashton school.

After passing Hill Farm and through a small coppice, the Way cuts across fields to veer left at a barn and right past a cottage. Crossing Hall Lane and a cattle grid, the route ascends steeply, crossing the fields at an angle to Langridge Lane then following the fence and wall to the Granville Monument south-west of The Battlefields.

The monument was erected by Lord Lansdown to honour the part his grandfather, Sir Bevil Granville, played in the Battle of Lansdown, fought on and around this hill on 5 July 1643. Bath, held by the Parliamentarians, was under threat of attack by the Royalists, so the city governor took his army to the strategic point at the top of Lansdown. After a skirmish at the base of the hill the Royalists, led by Sir Bevil Granville, pursued the Roundheads up the hill and stormed the scarp defence, to be met by a full bombardment of cannon shot. Granville charged on, leading his men forward causing the Parliamentarians to take refuge behind the stalwart Cotswold stone walls. Granville was mortally wounded and carried to Cold Ashton where he died. His troops did not press home the advantage they had gained, and many were killed the next day in an ambush. However, they mustered sufficiently to capture the city within two weeks.

The Way now goes along the track to a stile in the fence, then right along the road, then left to the monitoring station. Keeping to the right, aim straight towards the trig point on Hanging Hill. From here look backward at the landmarks passed along the Way – Cold Ashton bleakly on its hill to the right; the monuments on the knolls of Hawkesbury and Nibley; the spur of Stinchcombe beyond and the creases, crevices and combes indenting the scarp in between. To the west is the great spread of Bristol to where the trade flowed from the hills as horizons widened, with the Forest of Dean beyond, frowned upon by the distant peaks of Wales.

# 19

# Hanging Hill to Bath

Leaving Hanging Hill the Way angles off left on a path which skirts the golf course. By following the markers alongside the wood, the extreme westerly tip of the Cotswold escarpment is reached in open countryside at Little Down. This is the last of the hillforts on the Way – a stile points the route across it, then take a right turn onto the entrenchment. Waymarks direct you to a stile at the starting point of Bath Racecourse. Continue following the scarp line to Prospect Stile to view the next point of the Walk – Kelston Round Hill with its tuft of trees riding the summit.

Dropping down from Prospect Stile plateau, through fields, to skirt Kelston Hill, the Way angles left down Dean Hill to Pendean Farm. From Penn Hill, the final hill of the Way, we could see our goal and the full stop to our Walk – Bath. From our vantage point it was a swirl of honey and cream in a wooded bowl, the pinnacles of the abbey rising majestically above the tracery of trees and rooflines, the windwashed terraces of houses – sweeping statements of stone – riding the crescents of the green hillsides.

But we were not yet quite in the city. Weston, downhill from Penn Hill, bears little resemblance to the village from which it has grown to become an extension of Bath. It is entered by way of the recreation ground, Pennhill Road, and Anchor Road, to ascend Church Road. St Alphage was born here when it was a Saxon village, and rose in monastic prominence to become Archbishop of Canterbury, and a prisoner of some importance to the Danish invaders who finally stoned him to death. All Saints church, rebuilt in Victorian times, stands on the site of the Saxon church and the original village. Dr William Oliver is remembered here on a memorial, and on the plain biscuit he invented as an antidote to the rich food of eighteenth-century Bath; Samuel Purlewent, an eminent attorney, is remembered for his extraordinary funeral. He stipulated that none of his relatives should be present, only a dozen poor villagers who received half a guinea and a splendid dinner of beef and plum pudding for being merry and cheerful and refraining from 'weeping, crying, snivelling and

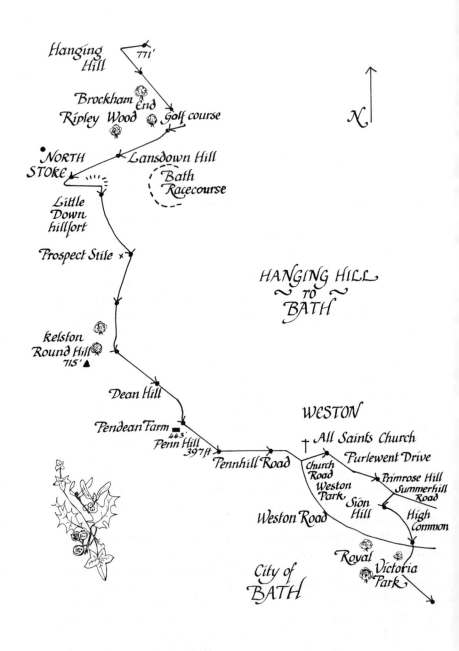

Hanging Hill

771'

Brockham End

Ripley Wood

Golf course

N

NORTH STOKE

Lansdown Hill

Bath Racecourse

Little Down hillfort

Prospect Stile ×

HANGING HILL
~ TO ~
BATH

Kelston Round Hill 715' ▲

Dean Hill

Pendean Farm
443'
Penn Hill 397ft

Pennhill Road

WESTON

† All Saints Church

Purlewent Drive

Church Road
Weston Park

Primrose Hill
Summerhill Road

Sion Hill

High Common

Weston Road

Royal Victoria Park

City of
BATH

the like'. His name is perpetuated in the housing estate's Purlewent Drive, into which the route continues on its way to a squeeze stile, with its big-boot bottom. Climb the steps of Primrose Hill and enter Summerhill Road. A left turn into Sion Hill road leads to a tree-lined path between the High Common and the golf course. Royal Victoria Park, which is entered on its north side, has one of the finest collections of trees in the country, and over five thousand different varieties of plants in its botanical gardens with a view of Royal Crescent sweeping away in elegant stone symmetry.

We entered Bath on the shortest day of the year, so we took what we considered the shortest route to the abbey. From the Victoria monument through a sphinx-guarded gateway, we went into Royal Avenue. Royal Crescent to the left, is the architectural masterpiece of John Wood the Younger, and the first of its kind in England. Sir Isaac Pitman settled down at No 17 after he left Wotton-under-Edge, and Sheridan the playwright eloped from No 11 with Elizabeth Linley. From the Royal Avenue, a left turn into Queen Square, then right, brings one into the bottom end of Gay Street; Josiah Wedgwood, founder of the famous English pottery, lived at No 30. Proceeding south into Barton Street, go down Sawclose. Popjoy's is where Beau Nash lived with his mistress, Juliana Popjoy, who, after his death, left the house and lived in a hollow tree.

Richard 'Beau' Nash ruled Regency Bath with flamboyance and flair. A quixotic character, his undistinguished background led to an undistinguished career at Oxford and in law; through luck and sheer audacity he assumed an authority over the life of the city unmatched anywhere else. Five years after Nash settled in Bath, a Cornishman called Ralph Allen took the job as assistant to the postmistress. In gratitude for his development of the major postal routes across England, he received what was then a small fortune which he invested in quarrying the hitherto despised Bath stone from Combe Down. He then attracted the architects John Wood, the Elder and Younger, to raise the honey-coloured stone in distinguished Palladian style to create a classical city. Nash, Allen and the Woods left a legacy of society legend and stone beauty which it takes time to explore in detail.

From Sawclose, turning left into Westgate Street and on to Cheap Street brings one to the heart of the great city. We had coffee and Bath buns in the elegant Georgian pump room, hung

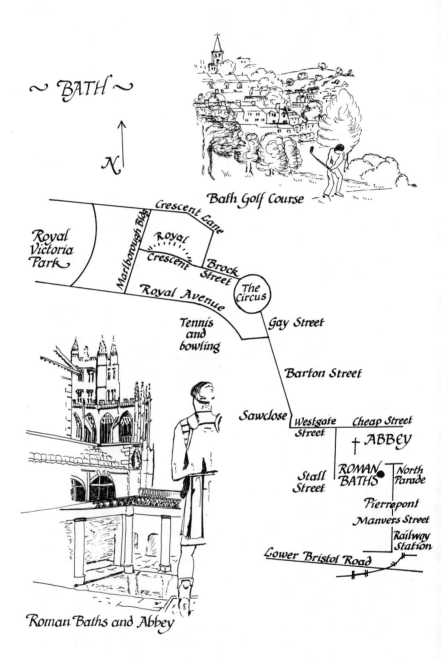

~ BATH ~

N

Bath Golf Course

Royal Victoria Park

Marlborough Bldg

Crescent Lane

Royal Crescent

Brock Street

Royal Avenue

The Circus

Gay Street

Tennis and bowling

Barton Street

Sawclose

Westgate Street

Cheap Street

† ABBEY

Stall Street

ROMAN BATHS

North Parade

Pierrepont

Manvers Street

Railway Station

Lower Bristol Road

Roman Baths and Abbey

around with evergreens, the lilting music from the young trio rising and mingling with the tinkling of coffee cups. We sank deep into the grace of the eighteenth century, glowing with achievement and hot strong coffee; the snowy-white tablecloth hid our walking boots. At our neighbouring table Eric Sykes, the television star, joked with the mayor about parking problems and his role in Bath's pantomine, *Dick Whittington*. We exchanged proud smiles, for it was the story of our Gloucestershire lad – a fitting follow-through, we thought, to our journey.

We toured the ancient Roman baths, the steam from the constantly hot waters rising in the crisp winter air, the smell of iron on hot stone lingering between the massive masonry; we marvelled at the bronze beauty of Minerva and the fierce face of the Gorgon, and the way of life lived here at Aquae Sulis two thousand years ago. The last programme had already been broadcast. Outside the baths, with a street-theatre group strutting on stilts to the merriment of a crowd bristling with shopping, a morose young guitarist moaning about the injustices of the world, and the strain of a Salvation Army band carolling on the corner, Nen had conversed into the BBC microphone on the phenomena of the hot springs that had stained the stones a rich red from 10,000 years unceasing flow and constant temperature that had given Bath its name and fame.

I had spoken about the abbey, its magnificence matched only by its long history. For in all the beauty that is Bath, it is the abbey that holds central stage – a fitting climax to an almost 100 mile (160km) walk.

Wax-red berried holly, carol sheets and bright-eyed choristers were being assembled as we took another look around its memorial-lined ancient walls.

Outside the abbey, lights flickered on to illuminate the street decorations, Father Christmas blew on his blue hands rattling a collection box, and shoppers turned up their collars against the sudden chill. We sought out the oldest house in Bath for tea with a Sally Lunn. Frost sparkled on the cobbled alleyways as we peered at pretty things in shop windows as Jane Austen and her sister must have done in their day. The last vestige of daylight glowed wanly pink over the hills above the city.

The day, the year, almost ended; the walk completed. We still had mud on our boots, but a song in our hearts, for we were lucky; we were going home – the Cotswold Way.

# Cotswold Calendar

Annual events on or within five miles of the Cotswold Way route.

MARCH
**National Hunt Festival, Cheltenham**   Includes the Queen Mother Champion Chase and coveted Gold Cup.

APRIL
**Badminton Three-day Horse Trials**

MAY
*Sunday*, The first
**Cheese-rolling at Randwick**   Three cheeses are rolled round the village church. One is then cut up and distributed, the others are kept for the 'Runnick' Wap (see next entry).

*Saturday*, The second (afternoon)
**Wap and Mayor-making ceremony, Randwick**   Cheese-rolling. Mayor elected and chaired from the Wap to Mayor's Pool in procession with May Queen and full retinue of High Sheriff and Flagman, having been voted into office by freeholders who have signed the Poll Book. The Mayor's cup is filled in the local pub and handed round in the evening.

*Spring Bank Holiday*: Monday (evening)
**Cheese-rolling down Cooper's Hill**   A competition which continues a tradition of at least four hundred years, commemorating the time when local folk put forward their rights to graze the commonland and a cheese was rolled down this precipitous gradient.

*Spring Bank Holiday*: Friday following (evening)
**Dover's Games** on Dover's Hill and **Torchlight Procession** to Chipping Campden.

*Spring Bank Holiday*: Saturday following (afternoon and evening)
**Scuttlebrook Wake** in Chipping Campden.

MAY–JUNE
**Bath International Festival of Music and the Arts** (founded in 1947)   Details from early March from Bath Festival office, Linley House, 1 Pierrepont Place, Bath. Tel: Bath 64431

JULY
**Cheltenham Festival of Music**   Details from Town Hall, Cheltenham, Gloucestershire, or Tourist Office.

*Sunday* of, or after, 19 (afternoon)
**Clipping Ceremony** at St Mary's Church, Painswick 'Clipping' in this ceremony means embracing. The clergy and choir are led by a local band in procession round the churchyard of the ninety-nine yew trees to the hymn 'Brightly gleams our banner'. The children with garlands of flowers in their hair join hands round the church and as they, and the congregation, sing the traditional Clipping Hymn 'Daily, daily sing the praises', they raise their arms and surge towards the church at the chorus of: O, that I had wings of Angels. After the service the children are presented with a Painswick bun and a coin.

OCTOBER
**Cheltenham Festival of Literature** Details from Town Hall, Cheltenham, Gloucestershire, or Tourist Office.

**Stroud Festival** Music, literature, drama and art. Details from Tourist Office.

CHRISTMAS-TIDE – **Mumming Plays** The mumming play is an ancient pagan ritual based on the death of winter personified in a fight between evil and good characters.

**Waterley Bottom Mummers** Dursley, Cam, Wotton-under-Edge district from about 22 December.

**City of Gloucester Mummers** Cheltenham and Gloucester. Boxing Day.

**Marshfield Mummers** Unique 'paper boys'; Boxing Day.

ACTUAL DATES AND VENUES Local Tourist Offices, local press or in 'Diary Events' of *Cotswold Life* or *Gloucestershire and Avon*.

# Places of Interest on or within 5 miles of the Cotswold Way

NT National Trust
HB Historic Buildings and Monuments Commission

*Note*: Charges (where applicable) have been omitted as prices become out-dated.

CHIPPING CAMPDEN AND DISTRICT
**Woolstapler's Hall**, High Street, Chipping Campden, Glos. (Tel: Evesham 840289)

Country bygones and social history including photographic and cine-

matographic collections, housed in old woolstapler's house.
*Open*: April to September daily 1100–1800 and October weekends.

**Campden Car Collection**, High Street, Chipping Campden, Glos. (Tel: Evesham 840289)

Collection of historic sports cars 1927–1963.
*Open*: April to September 1400–1800

**Ernest Wilson Memorial Garden**, Leysbourne, off High Street, Chipping Campden, Glos.

Small garden of the plants of a great Victorian garden and plant collector. List of plants available from the Tourist Office, Woolstapler's Hall.
*Open*: daylight hours throughout the year.

**Hidcote Manor Garden (NT)**, Hidcote Bartrim, Nr Chipping Campden, Glos. (Tel: Mickleton 333); 4 miles (6.4km) north-east of Chipping Campden

A garden of gardens – breathtaking. Summer Shakespeare production staged on Theatre Lawn. Details from NT, Tewkesbury. Refreshments in tearoom. No picnics.
*Open*: daily April to end October 1100–2000 except Tuesday and Friday (closed Good Friday).

**Kiftsgate Court Gardens**, 3 miles (4.8km) north-east of Chipping Campden, Glos.

Famous for its roses; lovely setting.
*Open*: April to September – Wednesday, Thursday and Sunday 1400–1800

BROADWAY TO STANWAY
**Fish Hill Picnic Site**, Broadway, Worcs.

Picnic area and nature trails.

**Broadway Tower Country Park, Worcs.** (Tel: Broadway 852390)

Exhibitions on the Cotswold wool trade and work of William Morris staged in the Tower. Country classroom, nature trails and adventure playground. Café/restaurant, picnic and barbecue areas
*Open*: April to early October 1000–1800

**Snowshill Manor (NT)**, Worcs. (Tel: Broadway 852410); 3 miles (4.8km) south-west of Broadway

Extensive collection ranging from musical instruments to 'a Hundred Wheels', arranged in a traditional Cotswold manor house set in terraced garden.

*Open*: April and October – Saturday, Sunday and Easter Monday, 1100–1300 and 1400–1700, May to end September – Wednesday to Sunday and Bank Holiday Monday 1100–1300 and 1400–1800.

**Buckland Rectory**, Worcs. (Tel: Broadway 852479); 1½ miles (2.4km) from Broadway

One of England's oldest rectories. Medieval house with fifteenth-century great hall.
*Open*: May to July – Mondays, 1100–1600; August – Mondays and Fridays 1100–1600

**Stanway House**, Stanway, Glos (Tel: Stanton 469)

Jacobean manor set in a charming parkland village.
*Open*: June, July and August – Tuesday and Thursday 1400–1700. Teas at Old Bakehouse in the village.

WINCHCOMBE AND DISTRICT
**Hailes Abbey (HB)**, Glos. (Tel: HB Bristol Office 734472)

Extensive ruins of thirteenth-century Cistercian abbey. Excellent museum depicting the history of Hailes.
*Open*: 15 March to 15 October – Monday–Saturday 0930–1830; Sunday 1400–1830. 16 October to 14 March – Monday–Saturday 0930–1600; Sunday 1400–1600

**Winchcombe Museum**, High Street corner of North Street, Winchcombe, Glos. (Tel: Winchcombe 602925)

Local artefacts, including finds from Belas Knap. Police uniforms and items from all over the world
*Open*: Monday to Saturday 1000–1700

**Winchcombe Railway Museum**, 23 Gloucester Street, Winchcombe, Glos. (Tel: Winchcombe 602257)

*Open*: seasonal variations – safer to enquire.

**Sudeley Castle**, Winchcombe, Glos. (Tel: Winchcombe 602308)

Medieval castle, home to Catherine Parr, the sixth wife and widow of Henry VIII, which contains Europe's largest private collection of toys. Exhibitions. Refreshments in the Old Kitchen.
*Open*: Castle – April to October daily 1200–1700. Grounds – 1100–1730. Falconry displays – May to August; Wednesday, Thursday and Sunday

**Cotswold Farm Park**, Guiting Power, Cheltenham, Glos. (Tel: Guiting 307); about 3 miles (4.8km) from Winchcombe

Britain's largest collection of rare breed animals in farmland setting, including 'Cotswold Lions'. Refreshments. Picnic area.
*Open*: May to September; 1030–1800 daily

**Postlip Hall**, Glos.; 1 mile (1.6km) south of Winchcombe off the A46 (Tel: T. Stevenson, Cheltenham 45533 – office hours; or 603187 – evenings and weekends)

Gabled Cotswold manor house dating back to the fifteenth century. Privately owned but the Hall and grounds are often open for cultural events and exhibitions.

PAINSWICK AND STROUD DISTRICT
**Crickley Hill Country Park**, Glos.

On site is one of the most important archaeological hillforts dating back to eary Neolithic times. Display area; trails and guided tours available. For information on the Crickley Hill Trust, excavation dates and lecture programmes contact Mrs M. Imlah, Crickley Hill Project, c/o Westbury House, Lansdown Road, Cheltenham, Glos. or the Sites Warden (Tel: Gloucester 20113) or Head Cotswold Warden (Tel: Gloucester 425674)

**Cooper's Hill Local Nature Reserve**, Glos.; 3 miles (4.8km) north of Painswick on Cotswold Way route. General enquiries: Sites Warden (Tel: Gloucester 20113) or Head Cotswold Warden (Tel: Gloucester 425674)

Nature trail with points of archaeological interest.

**Prinknash Abbey**, Cranham, Glos. (Tel: Painswick 812239); ½ mile (.8km) off the Cotswold Way from Cranham Corner – on the A46

World-famous pottery; viewing gallery open Monday to Saturday 1030–1630; Sunday 1300–1630. Gift Shop; tearoom 0930–1730 daily; monastery garden selling plants, produce in season. Guided tours by arrangement.

**Court House**, Painswick, Glos. (Tel: Painswick 873689)

Court room, circa 1610, with Civil War associations.
*Open*: weekdays by appointment

**Painswick House**, Glos. (Tel: Painswick 813646)

A fine Palladian house.
*Open*: July to September – weekends and Bank Holidays, 1400–1800

**Stroud Museum**, Lansdown Road, Stroud, Glos. (Tel: Stroud 3394)

Extensive collection from prehistoric times, with emphasis on local geology industry.
*Open*: Monday to Saturday 1030–1300 and 1400–1700

**Coaley Peak**, Glos.

Picnic area with nature trails and information centre. General enquiries: Sites Warden (Tel: Gloucester 20113) or Head Warden (Tel: Gloucester 425674)

**Frocester Tithe Barn**, Frocester Court, Nr Stonehouse, Stroud, Glos. (Tel: Stonehouse 3250); about 1 mile (1.6km) from Coaley Peak picnic area

Tithe barn close to Tudor gatehouse and courthouse.
*Open*: throughout the year at reasonable daytime hours

BERKELEY AND DURSLEY
**Berkeley Castle**, Glos. (Tel: Dursley 810332); 4½ miles (7.2km) from Dursley

Home of the Berkeley family since 1153.
*Open*: seasonal changes – safer to enquire.

**The Jenner Museum**, The Chantry, High Street, Berkeley, Glos. (Tel: Dursley 810631); 4 miles (6.4km) from Dursley

Fine collection of Dr Jenner's pioneer work on smallpox vaccination housed in his old home.
*Open*: daily (except Monday) 1100–1730

**Owlpen Manor**, Owlpen, Dursley, Glos. (Tel: Dursley 860261); 2 miles (3.2km) from Dursley

Charming Tudor manor house with a rare set of seventeenth-century painted cloth wall-hangings, in a group with court house, church and grist mill.
*Open*: May to September by written appointment only.

**Wildfowl Trust**, Slimbridge, Glos. (Tel: Dursley 89333); 4 miles (6.4km) from Dursley

Largest collection of wildfowl in the world in acres of lovely grounds. Refreshments and picnic areas.
*Open*: Throughout the year (excluding Christmas) 0930–1600

HORTON AND DYRHAM
**Horton Court** (NT), Horton, Avon; 3 miles (4.8km) north-east of Chipping Sodbury

Norman hall with interesting collection ranging from armour to bicycles; ambulatory in the garden.
*Open*: April to October – Wednesday and Saturday 1400–1800 or sunset if earlier.

**Dyrham Park** (NT), Avon; Dyrham, Nr Chippenham, Wilts (Tel: Abson 2501)

Entrance Lodge on A46 (2 miles (3.2km) south of M4 – Exit 18). Mansion built 1691–1702, furnished closely as recorded in the housekeeping inventory of that time, set in beautiful parkland where deer have roamed since Saxon times.
*Open*: House and garden – April, May and October daily (except

Thursday and Friday) 1400–1800; June to end September daily (except Friday) 1400–1800 or dusk if earlier.
Park – all the year 1200–1800, or dusk if earlier. Tea in the Orangery. Picnics welcome. National Trust members please announce your name at the door for access from the back through the church.

# Tourist Information

AC = Area covered by Accommodation Lists.

**Bath** (Avon)
Director of Leisure and Tourist Services, Pump Room, Bath, BA1 1LZ (Tel: Bath 61111) general, (Bath 60521) accommodation
AC: Bath and area

**Cheltenham** (Glos)
61 Promenade (Tel: Cheltenham 522878)
AC: most of Gloucestershire and the Cotswolds

**Chipping Campden** (Glos)
Woolstapler's Hall (Tel: Evesham 840289)
AC: immediate area

**Cirencester** (Glos)
Cornhall, Market Place (Tel: Cirencester 4180)
AC: area extends to Moreton-in-Marsh, Fairford, Stroud and Tetbury

**Gloucester**
6 College Street (Tel: Gloucester 421188)
AC: Gloucestershire and the Cotswolds

**Stroud** (Glos)
High Street (Tel: Stroud 4252)
AC: Stroud and district extending to Dursley and Berkeley

**Winchcombe** (Glos)
High Street Corner, off North Street (Tel: Winchcombe 602925)
AC: immediate area

# Travel Information

## Getting to the Cotswold Way by Public Transport

**Train services**: connect to Bath, Stroud, Cheltenham, Moreton-in-Marsh and Evesham from London and/or Birmingham.

*Enquiries*: time-tables and Golden Rail holidays on lines serving the Cotswolds: Worcester–Tel: 27211; Oxford 722333; Gloucester 29501

**National Express coaches**: connect to Bath, Cheltenham, Stroud and Broadway.

**Bus services**: Local bus companies serving the Cotswold Way are as follows. Enquire direct for details.

National Express, Coach Station, St Margaret's Road, Cheltenham, Glos (Tel: 38331).

Barry's Coaches, Pool Garage, Moreton-in-Marsh, Glos (Tel: 50876)

Cresswell, High Street, Broadway, Worcs (Tel: Evesham 853433)

Castleways Coaches, Castle House, Greet Road, Winchcombe, Glos (Tel: 602949/603715)

Marchants Coaches, 433/7 High Street, Cheltenham, Glos (Tel: 22714)

Pulham & Sons (Coaches) Ltd, Station Road, Bourton-on-the-Water, Glos (Tel: 20369)

Bristol Omnibus Co Ltd, Berkeley House, Lawrence Hill, Bristol.
   *Tel Enquiries* (office hours): Cheltenham 22021; Gloucester 27516; Stroud 3421/2; Bath 64446; Bristol 558211

Westward Travel, 10 The Chipping, Kingswood, Wotton-under-Edge, Glos (Tel: Dursley 842453)

National Bus Co, Coach Station, St Margaret's Road, Cheltenham, Glos (Tel: 511655)

Midland Red (South) Ltd, Warwick Road, Stratford-upon-Avon, Warcs (Tel: 204181) Head Office: Railway Terrace, Rugby, Warcs (Tel: Rugby 62036) *Note*: Seasonal only. Additional Cotswold tour programmes also available.

Fosseway Coaches, The Post Office, Grittleton, Wilts (Tel: Castle Combe 78401)

Gloucestershire County Council, Shire Hall, Gloucester (Tel: 21444 Ext 490)

Swanbrook Transport, Thomas House, St Margaret's Road, Cheltenham, Glos (Tel: 32591)

Midland Red (West) Ltd, 7 Edgar Street, Worcester (Tel: Evesham 2515)

*A Bus and Rail Guide to the Cotswolds* is published annually by Gloucestershire County Council. It is obtainable from The Surveyors' Dept, Shire Hall, Gloucester (Tel: 21444 Ext 7619) and includes ideas for voluntary car schemes, community mini-bus schemes and club transport.

# Acknowledgements

I am grateful to the many people who have so readily answered my questions, and proved so helpful along the Way.

Thanks are due to Mr J. S. Maitland for details of Lister's of Dursley; Marling and Evans of Stanley Mills; Lord Neidpath of Stanway House and Father Aldhelm Cameron-Brown, Abbot of Prinknash. Especial thanks to Ted Fryer, head warden of the Cotswold warden service for checking my route maps and for answering my innumerable questions; Carole Fleetwood who administers the mountain of paper work, and fellow wardens David Jelfs and Cyril Trenfield.

Thanks too to George Hart (Jethro Larkin of *The Archers*) for allowing me to use his name and refer to our recording, and to the BBC for permission to use the relevant extracts. And to Caroline Elliot, senior producer of BBC Outside Broadcasts, for giving up her weekends to walk some of the Way with us for *The Countryside* programmes, and especially for her interest and good wishes.

To Nen, my special gratitude for not only walking the ninety-seven and a half miles with me, but for her constant help in everything from scraping the Cotswold mud off my boots to typing my manuscript.

# Index